SKIDDING *into* HEAVEN

SUZANNE MURRAY

SKIDDING *into* HEAVEN

DEFYING DEATH, DIVORCE, AND DISEASE WITH UNWAVERING FAITH

Contact information for Tulip Books Publishing 2040 S Alma Sch RD PMB497 Chandler, AZ 85286

ISBN: 979-8-9896529-0-7 (paperback)
ISBN: 979-8-9896529-1-4 (ebook)
ISBN: 979-8-9896529-2-1 (hardcover)
ISBN: 979-8-9896529-3-8 (audiobook)

Ordering Information:
Special discounts are available on quantity purchases by corporations, associations, and others. For details, contact info@suzannemurrayauthor.com

Publisher's Cataloging-in-Publication Data
Names: Murray, Suzanne, 1954- .
Title: Skidding into heaven : defying death, divorce, and disease with unwavering faith / Suzanne Murray.
Description: Chandler, AZ : Tulip Books Publishing, 2024. | Summary: Memoir of a woman facing life challenges including death, divorce, and a cancer diagnosis with hope, good humor, and resiliency.
Identifiers: ISBN 9798989652921 (hardback) | ISBN 9798989652907 (pbk.) | ISBN 9798989652914 (ebook) | ISBN 9798989652938 (audiobook)
Subjects: LCSH: Murray, Suzanne, 1954- . | Divorced women – United States – Biography. | Cancer – Patients – Biography. | Bereavement. | Positive psychology. | Hope. | Faith. | BISAC: BIOGRAPHY & AUTOBIOGRAPHY / Memoirs. | BIOGRAPHY & AUTOBIOGRAPHY / Women. | BIOGRAPHY & AUTOBIOGRAPHY / Medical.
Classification: LCC CT275.M87.A3 2024 | DDC 920.72 M--dc23

DEDICATION

To all who encouraged me to write my story,

This book is a testament to the power of support and the strength that comes from having a community that believes in you. From the depths of my heart, I dedicate these words to each and every one of you who inspired, cheered, and urged me to share my God-inspired stories with the world.

If you have an inspiring story, please send me an email at suzanne@suzannemurrayauthor.com.

ACKNOWLEDGMENTS

While writing this book, I have been fortified by my unwavering faith in God, who has been my constant source of comfort and trust during countless crises. His boundless love and guidance have provided solace and strength, inspiring me to persevere even in the face of adversity. I acknowledge God's divine presence as the anchor that steadies my pen and gives purpose to my words.

I must also extend my heartfelt appreciation to my family, whose unwavering support and presence have been the bedrock of my life. Through both the joys and trials that come with writing, they have stood by my side, providing encouragement and understanding. Their love has been a wellspring of inspiration, fueling my determination to share this journey with the world.

To God and my cherished family, I offer my deepest gratitude. Your contributions and steadfastness have been pivotal to the creation of this book. May your involvement in this endeavor be a testament to the power of collaboration, faith, and love in shaping a work that I hope will resonate with readers for generations to come.

I am profoundly grateful to Nancy Burkhalter, whose exceptional expertise in crafting words has been instrumental in shaping this nonfiction book. Her talent for weaving an enthralling narrative has brought life to the pages and enriched the reader's experience in ways beyond measure. Nancy's dedication and passion for storytelling have been an invaluable asset throughout this creative journey.

TABLE OF CONTENTS

INTRODUCTION

I'm just like you. I have worked hard all my life, paid my taxes, and played by the rules. But also like you, I've gone through some pretty tough times—physically, financially, and emotionally. Any one of them could have done me in and caused me to give up. But they haven't. And that's what this book is about.

I may die soon. I have cancer...for the second time. But this time it's Stage 4. Nevertheless, I am at peace with it. The silver lining is that it has made me taste and feel and see each day as if for the first time. I listen to the robins singing in my yard with a renewed sense of awe. I take in the earthy scent of the soil as I plant my carrots and cucumbers. I hug each of my 13 grandchildren as if for the last time. I kiss my beloved husband as often as I can. The good Lord saw fit to send him to me late in life. What a gift.

I have no doubt that each of you has experienced blessings interlaced with hard times. But what is life if not a journey, right? We jockey the twists and turns, relish the sweet surprises, and survive the heavy hardships as best we can. Let me share my path through it all. Come laugh and weep with me as I recount how I struggled—and still do—to make sense out of this wacky world. I will show you how to giggle at your own battles, and best of all, share how God has been my mainstay, my rock, my cuddly blanket during my many dark days. Because of my faith, I have never felt alone.

I believe that you will find solace in this book, which is for anyone who has been treated badly or endured the death of a loved one or even battled a life-threatening disease. Whatever your burden, I can relate because they've all happened to me.

I can say without hesitation that when I depart these shores, I will have failed at a lot (I can't organize closets worth a darn) and have succeeded at a lot (I am a whiz at doing taxes). All of it I've done with passion and grit. I am satisfied that I've left it all on the field. But I'm not done yet. I want to travel abroad, see my children often, and dance under the stars every chance I get. There is no time to waste. I will have been so busy that when the time comes to leave this earth, I will skid into the gates of heaven. St. Peter will know it's me because I will have the biggest smile on my face.

I cling to my great hope, but no matter how many hardships I have overcome, facing death is a bit scary, I'll admit. In between those uncomfortable thoughts, though, I say to my husband, "Let's go somewhere and have some fun!" And off we go!

Let me show you not only what my challenges presented to

me, but how I have endured. I hope you can take heart from my struggles and may even see yourself in some.

Finally, I'm a terrific listener and would greatly appreciate hearing your stories about the challenges you have faced and ways of coping you have developed. I can always learn more.

Thank you for joining me on my journey. Godspeed to you.

suzanne@suzannemurrayauthor.com

CHAPTER 1

TURNING POINT—A NEAR-DEATH EXPERIENCE

I was 38 when I got pregnant with my third child, young enough to expect a normal pregnancy and birth, especially since I had had two others—Jarrod, four, and Alexis, two who would turn three on August 17. Both births were a breeze. But it did cross my mind that maybe, just maybe, I might be pushing my luck now. Little did I know how much I would push it.

When I was 14 weeks pregnant, my daughter Alexis (still two at the time) fell on some concrete. As I whisked her up and perched her on my left hip, I felt and heard a pop inside me. Uh-oh. Later that evening, I started slowly bleeding. The next morning, Jon, my husband, had to go out of town. I was making pancakes for the kids when the bleeding worsened. I got really scared.

I went to the hospital for an ultrasound, which showed a low-lying placenta that had torn just a little.

The bleeding continued. I didn't pay much attention to it, and neither did the doctors. When I was about six months along, though, and the bleeding didn't cease, they finally became concerned and ordered complete bedrest.

I chuckled under my breath. Bedrest and young kids don't mix. If you are a parent, you know it is almost impossible to totally check out of life when you have little ones running around asking for snacks and story time. It's a 24/7 job.

The situation was made worse because I'm a go-getter. I usually don't let things get in my way in life. So, against medical advice to lie around all day, I took my kids to daycare, went to work for a few hours, returned home to put my feet up, then picked up the kids, made dinner, and cleaned up. I don't know who I thought I was kidding, but my magical thinking was making things worse.

For the rest of the pregnancy, I bled every day. In my seventh month, an upsetting situation at work just about did me in. I was efficiently going about my business when the employee in the next office ran in and said, "Call 911! My wife is going to commit suicide!"

I called 911, but the dispatcher kept asking for information I didn't have. So, I kept having to run into his office to ask questions like "Does she have any weapons? Has she taken any pills? Is she near a window or ledge? Is anyone else at home?"

Thank goodness the police were able to get to her before anything happened. I, however, started bleeding rather heavily from that stress. When I got to the doctor's office, I was immediately taken to the hospital where they gave me drugs to stop labor.

Nothing worked. So, they loaded me into an ambulance bound for a more high-tech hospital.

There, I had an amniocentesis done to determine whether the baby's lungs were mature enough in case they had to deliver the baby. Yes, the lungs were mature. That finding was somewhat comforting. All of that happened on Wednesday.

Time dragged, but my stepdaughter, Dionne, visited me in the hospital. We passed the time by thinking of names for a boy or a girl. I was wearing a baby monitor to keep an eye on the baby's heart rate. The heartbeat began pounding really loud, like BAM! BAM! BAM! as the baby moved around. So, we picked the name Brittany Amber Murray for a girl and Blake Allan Murray for a boy, both initials were BAM.

By Saturday, August 17, the contractions had stopped. Crisis averted. So, I asked if I could go home to celebrate Alexis's third birthday. It was not to be. That morning, I got out of bed and bled all over the floor and bathroom. The doctors laid down the law: I was to stay in the hospital until the baby reached maturity in October. Since it was August, the news was very upsetting. I cried most of the morning while Dionne was at home creating a small birthday party for Alexis.

I was alone most of the time. Jon stayed Thursday and Friday nights with me, then went home on Saturday to be with the little ones and get some sleep. Dionne was out on a date and said she would check in later. She called at about midnight.

"I'm in labor again!" I told her.

I felt very comforted that she came to the hospital to be with me. She had attended the births of my other two children, which were natural. At this point, I was dilated to four centimeters and had six more to go before the baby could be born. Suddenly, I was in excruciating pain with gushing blood at each contraction.

Then the worst news of all: The baby's heart stopped beating.

I have only sketchy memories of the rest of the event, except for the excruciating pain.

A doctor listened for the baby's heartbeat. Still nothing.

At this point, I thought I was dying. Everything happened fast. I was taken headlong to the operating room. I remember them slamming the gurney against the doors at ramming speed. Now, I *knew* I was dying. The baby had no heartbeat. Every contraction was unbearable. I could hardly breathe. My placenta was completely abrupted, torn away from the uterine wall. Blood was everywhere. The loss of blood must have made me think that death was imminent.

There was no time for a Cesarean, so the doctor manually dilated me and started pulling the baby out. I remember an out-of-body experience where I was hovering above the bed and then went quickly down a river. I stopped abruptly and remembered feeling totally at peace from the inside out. It was so warm and comforting there. I remember floating but didn't see a garden or the Lord. There are no words powerful enough to describe the wonderful, engulfing feeling.

Right about then, Dionne told me later, the doctor ordered her to start screaming my name in my ear. I remember hearing her but wanted to stay where I was. Then, suddenly, I knew I had to go back.

The next thing I remember was being overwhelmed with joy. I was alive.

Finally delivered, my baby was rushed out of the OR so that they could revive the newborn. I didn't know I had had a girl, Brittany Amber Murray, until about an hour later when they returned and allowed me to see her for just a minute before they put her in the Neonatal Intensive Care Unit (NICU). I was finally given some drugs for pain. And, boy, did I sleep!

I still had to heal from the abruption, and Brittany had to get strong enough to come home. But thanks to the fast-acting ambulance guys, competent doctors, and the excellent nurses in the NICU, where "preemies" try to survive, there was a happy ending to what could have been a tragedy. The young doctor who was on call that night came to my room, sat on my bed, took my hands in his and said, "I am so glad this turned out the way it did with both of you alive." Me too, I whispered.

Still, a touch of sadness lingered beneath the joy I felt. Staying in the hospital was hard for me because I was in the maternity ward. I had to room with a number of other women who had their babies in the room. Not being able to have Brittany with me and hold her was so different from my previous two births. Envy and jealousy were constant emotions.

NICUs are off limits to almost everyone. Jon and I were only allowed to see our two-month premature baby, weighing all of four pounds and eight ounces, in that area, where she was hooked up to all kinds of monitors. She had an IV and was fed through a small tube. We had to fully scrub and gown to enter the NICU and could only put our hands through holes in the incubator to touch our miracle girl. If you've ever been in a NICU, you know it's noisy because alarms were constantly going off to alert the nurses when a baby stopped breathing.

Brittany was a fierce fighter in the NICU, just as she had been in utero. She and I both fought to get her out into the world, a battle we almost lost. Today, she's a gorgeous 31-year-old, who has a master's degree in psychology and is still scrappy as all get-out. Brittany worked for five years with domestic violence survivors. She is now working on her doctorate degree. She is smart and so caring. Because of the high-risk birth, the doctors did not want me to have any other children. Jon and I called Brittany our "miracle baby."

I remained in the hospital for several days after her birth. They wheeled a machine into my room (a double industrial-strength breast pump) so that I could give her breast milk. Because she was my third child, I had great milk ducts and could have fed a thousand babies. Let's hear it for multiple children!

A SECRET KEPT

I never told anyone about my out-of-body experience until years later. I thought I would be labeled as crazy. I hadn't had any drugs, so it was not a drug-induced experience. I've been told it was a near-death experience. I've read about others' experiences, and almost all of them talk about the same kind of eerie calm, whether it's seeing a white light or Jesus. Mine was a lightning-fast trip down a river. It scared me how close I came to continuing on that journey. As I reflect on the event, I am amazed I wasn't frantic about my precious son and daughter at home. For me at the time, however, the past and other concerns were not part of my experience.

There was no question in my mind that God had helped me through this crisis. I was minutes away from death with the amount of blood I was losing. How else can we explain when people come back from such dire circumstances?

Fast forward a bit to August 18, 1991. That day was the turning point in my life. It took that traumatic episode to help me get my priorities straight. It was also our 12th wedding anniversary. I acknowledged my blessing with renewed emphasis.

I began regularly attending a Lutheran church. I joined a women's Bible study group on Wednesdays. I even spent five years in Bible Study Fellowship that took an in-depth dive into the Bible. I oversaw all the leaders who taught the children. I studied the prophesies more in-depth and discovered that many of them have come true. Those choices got me more into my faith instead of being at work 60 hours a week. Work was not as important to me anymore. I decided I would never work 60 hours a week again. You never hear anyone facing death who says, "I wish I would have worked more."

Then, because I became so knowledgeable about the roots of Christianity, I traveled to Israel to visit the sacred places mentioned. I traced the steps that Jesus walked at the temple in Israel and saw the different archaeological sites mentioned in the scriptures. I also went to Ephesus in Turkey, the center of early Christianity. It all made my faith stronger because I could see where these events happened. I was even baptized in the Jordan River. I visited the area where a teenage shepherd found the Dead Sea Scrolls in the mid-1900s. He was tending his flock when he happened upon an opening in a cliff. Inside were clay jars containing leather and papyrus scrolls, 950 in all, written between 150 BC and AD 70. About a fourth of them are part of the Old Testament.[1] When I compared current writings with what had been written back then, the words were exactly the same. Mega goosebumps.

I also saw one of the fishing boats from the first century CE (Common Era). Known as the "Jesus Boat," it was discovered by the Sea of Galilee in 1986 in Israel.[2] A severe drought had left the boat

---

1 Joe Carter, "9 Things You Should Know About the Dead Sea Scrolls," The Gospel Coalition, March 22, 2021, https://www.thegospelcoalition.org/article/9-things-dead-sea-scrolls/.

2 Dan Fisher, "Israeli Archeologists Rush to Excavate 'Jesus Boat' From Sea of Galilee," *Los Angeles Times*, February 26, 1986, https://www.latimes.com/archives/la-xpm-1986-02-26-mn-54-story.html.

exposed in the mud. Two passersby found it and alerted a team of archaeologists who took great care to encase it in fiberglass and insulating foam during excavation to prevent further deterioration when it hit the air. This type of boat is mentioned 50 times in the Gospels.

I came away from these experiences with a profound connection to God and my faith in general. All the people and places and events came alive for me.

Not so for everyone, though. There is a letter St. Paul wrote to the Colossians that he also requested to be read to the people in Laodicea (further noted in Revelation 3:14-22) in which he warns the people that they have become complacent and lukewarm in their faith and had forgotten Jesus. I went to see the ruins of Ephesus in Turkey, which is not too far from Laodicea. Their houses were much bigger than those of the other ruins. They also had a vacation spot, Pamukkale, on a high hill that had summer breezes and beautiful white calcium on the sides of the hill with blue water pools in places.

The books I'd read about the people of Ephesus didn't do them justice. I could not compare anything to experiencing the water, the earth, the rocks they must have touched. I felt the wind and sun on my face and relished the surrounding beauty. But I also understood much more keenly the hardships the society faced, as well as the physical and probably emotional obstacles endured by the people. They must have felt the same contradiction in their lives.

Still, the passivity described in Paul's letter reminded me of the people in the U.S. today. For the most part we have so much, compared to other people in the world. But I believe we have become lukewarm and complacent about God. Jesus taught that we should love God and love people. We have become more about "me" and less about others, unfortunately.

Surely, He "speaks" to us *if* we listen. Sometimes, He delivers an extra loud wake-up call. In the search for meaning in life, people say that God tests them from time to time. They think that He is asking, "Just how deep is your faith?" Many people have met situations worse than mine. Certainly, soldiers in wartime come to mind. Their situations must have seemed apocalyptic, fraught with too much emotion at the time to absorb the import of the plight. The aftermath, too, can be hell to grasp. In my own ways, I have been there, folks. Several times. And without my faith, I may well have broken in two.

God tested me before my faith deepened and afterward. I don't know if He has a sense of humor. Looking back, I think He probably does, but it's only apparent in retrospect.

Take, for example, what happened when my neighbor Linda hosted a Bible study in our neighborhood for nine years. The participants kept a prayer journal to record how many of our prayers had been answered. In one case, we really got results, as well as a sign of God's sense of humor.

One of the members in our Bible study group had a daughter who wanted to get pregnant over Christmas while her husband was home from duty in Afghanistan. So, our Bible study group prayed and prayed, asking God to let her get pregnant. We may have overdone it. She ended up with twins! God does have a sense of humor.

CHAPTER 2

FAITH—THE BULWARK OF MY LIFE

Religion has always been in my family, but it did not come front and center in my life until I had my near-death experience giving birth to Brittany.

As the second of six kids, we were raised Lutheran in Seattle, Washington. We attended Sunday school, Bible study, church suppers, picnics, confirmation classes at 13 years old, baptisms, funerals, marriages—all the usual activities for families who enjoyed the warm embrace of Lutheran fellowship. We attended church every week.

Even with all those church activities—and there were a lot each month—I never had a personal relationship with God. A lot of my friends waxed eloquent about their intimate connection with God. I never felt that God was walking with me as they described it.

What did it feel like, I wondered, to be that close to God? Why didn't I feel that way? Is there something wrong with me?

I'm sure my Sunday school teachers talked about the intensity of that feeling at some point. None of it stuck. I figured those feelings would come in time, but until my near-death experience, the connection never meant anything to me. It seemed to be something to strive for, but how? Did it happen all of a sudden? If I read the Bible more? If I prayed more often? What, exactly, should I do?

Don't get me wrong. I loved God and obeyed the Bible's teaching as best I could, flawed human that I am. I also credit my religious upbringing for making me a positive, kind, sensitive human being. But this personal relationship with God was something vague and elusive, an idea that I didn't think I needed because I believed that following the tenets of Lutheranism was enough. For instance, we believe that all who repent their sins and accept Christ as their Savior are saved and can enter heaven, that there is a Triune God, the Father, Son, and Holy Ghost. Those tenets further state that each person can have a direct relationship with God. It is just between you and the Almighty.

It's funny, thinking back now on those many sermons I listened to that touched on this topic. I'd nod my head and *thought* I knew what the pastor was saying. If I am a believer, I will be okay, no matter what happens on earth. I am promised eternal life in heaven with God. These beliefs always comforted me, but I still didn't know how to *walk* with God. The urgency was never there to strive for that relationship.

The wonderful thing about religion is that it teaches us lessons we didn't even know we wanted or needed, like the one about courage. Take, for example, the story of Martin Luther.

Over 700 years ago, he nailed his 95 theses to the door of the Castle Church in Wittenberg, Germany, criticizing the Catholic church's selling of indulgences. Indulgences were never supposed to be sold or purchased. Their sole purpose was to reduce the time their loved ones would spend in purgatory before moving on to heaven.

In staid opposition, Luther didn't want believers to think they could buy their way into heaven. Today, we know how preposterous the idea is to think that people would be so gullible as to spend their meager income on a chance to buy a dwelling in heaven, a place they couldn't see but had heard the church say so much about.

As with all things in history up through today, though, I know better than to feel superior to anyone. But Martin Luther's story makes me admire him even more because of his ability to see reality more clearly and sidestep the greed of his own church. Luther must have had a boatload of courage to go up against the all-powerful Catholics. He risked it all—even his life—for his views, which were condemned as heretical. I am humbled at his courage.

These days, I aim to have a continual personal relationship with God. I love my religion. I now attend a nondenominational Bible-based church. It makes sense to me, and I feel empowered by the power of God's true word and the community provided by my church. But mostly, I internalized the lesson of the immense courage it took Luther to confront the mighty (and corrupt) Catholic church at the time. That brave act alone earned my admiration. I am proud to be part of a church.

I have further internalized the strength and comfort of God in the face of adversity. And, boy, have I needed it. Adversity, it seems, has set up shop on my doorstep and knocked a little too often on my door. Thanks to my belief in God, I have faced down divorce, death, trickster men, nearly dying, and now, cancer—for the second time. This time might be the last bit of misfortune I'll have to grapple with. Very few people win the battle when it's gotten this far into our bodies.

You may think that contracting cancer, even once, was the catalyst for the deepening of my religious beliefs. It wasn't. (I'll tell you all about how I came to deepen my faith in the next chapter.)

Before my personal relationship with God, I was trying to control everything. That obsession led to anxiety, worry, and a sense of dread. Worry about the little things in life was constant. I felt I had to be in charge and had no backup for any of life's challenges.

When I started being closer to God, I became more content in any circumstance. I let many small concerns go. I felt that I could pray and talk to God at any time day or night and know that I had my heavenly father to understand me and give me wisdom on how to handle difficult situations.

Now throughout the day, I say "arrow prayers," which are quick, short sentences just talking to God about any concern. For example, when driving past a person begging on the side of the road, I simply ask God to help them with their needs. Realizing that I have a 24-hour counselor in God, I can relax, knowing I do not have to control everything.

Even in tough times, I have experienced how God used them to help me grow and be able to help others. Without an understanding of hard circumstances like divorce and death, I would not have been able to have true understanding and empathy for someone in that situation. Enduring the death of a spouse is not something you would ever want to experience, but without going through that fire, there would be no way to truly feel someone else's pain.

The gift my faith has given me is the absence of worry and constant fretting about having to fill a "hole," although what that hole was, I couldn't articulate. I have a contentment about events, my family, and my fate. Gone is the constant anxiety I felt in my stomach. I feel so free.

CHAPTER 3

CANCER^2

After I reached age 35, I dutifully scheduled yearly mammograms. It was not unusual to get called back for a second look, so I didn't think anything about going in for a second set of X-rays one Friday afternoon when I was 51. After the test, I sat and waited so they could make sure the pictures were good enough.

I waited.

And waited.

The technician came out and said, "The doc wants me to take a few more pictures. Nothing to worry about. They just want to make sure."

(Every woman who has had a mammogram will tell you it's like a car ran over her breast then backed up to see what it ran over! The good news is that the discomfort lasts only a few seconds.)

Back to the waiting room. After what seemed like hours, the doctor came out to tell me they needed to do a biopsy—right away!

It's nothing, Sue, I said to myself. Just stay calm.

After putting wires into my left breast, I was escorted to a room where a doctor did a cone biopsy, which removes a piece of tissue shaped like an ice-cream cone. It is one of several kinds of biopsies they can perform to diagnose suspicious-looking tissue.

Once the sample was taken, the doctor said, "If this comes back noncancerous, I won't believe it," meaning she was diagnosing me without even evaluating the sample. Disbelief and terror entered my brain. What a bummer way to find out I had breast cancer! That doctor must have slept through the course in bedside manner, I thought.

I was truly in shock. Somehow, I drove home, barely keeping myself together.

I must have had a stricken look on my face when I got into the house. "What's wrong, Mom?" one of the kids asked.

I sat on the stairs and said, "I'm pretty sure I have breast cancer." I knew I'd have to wait for the biopsy to be analyzed, but I was sure just from the doctor's comment.

I couldn't help crying, which got my girls crying. Jarrod wasn't there. He was in Arizona going to automotive repair school. Eventually, Brittany said, "What's going to happen to us?"

It was then I realized that my 15-minute pity party was over. I needed to be strong for my kids who had already lost their dad five years earlier. (The story of their dad, Jon, will be told later.)

"God knows I'm a single mom," I told them. "He knows our situation. I can't predict how this will turn out, but I know God will take care of us."

Finally, I got the official call from the doctor to come in. Yes, I had breast cancer. I immediately wanted to know my options. I told them I wanted to start treatment immediately. So, they scheduled me for a lumpectomy. Before surgery, they told me that if the radioactive contrast they injected showed no cancer in my lymph nodes, I could go home that day.

No such luck.

In the recovery room, I asked my daughters if they knew whether I had to stay overnight. They were both crying. "Yes, Mom. They said you do."

I was in a good amount of pain. I wasn't sure why because pain from lumpectomies is usually fairly mild. The doctor came in and told me what they had done while I was under anesthesia. "We had to take the lymph nodes out from under your left arm…I inserted a drain." He left the room so that I could sleep and told me we would talk the next day.

I soon became aware of feeling wet on that side but was too out of it to know why. When the nurse came into my room to do some procedure, she saw my bloody gown on the side of the operation. Apparently, the stitches holding the drain in place had come undone. So, they had to stitch the drain back in place in my hospital room.

The lumpectomy surgery took place on November 8, 2005. We had a trip planned to Fort Lauderdale over Thanksgiving in a mere three weeks. I announced to the doctor we were going no matter what—drain or no drain. Such defiance was typical of my ignoring my pain and going about my life, problems be damned.

I'm sure he scowled at me and explained that the drain would need to come out while we were gone. "Okay," I said. "Just give me the surgical kit so I can have my daughter Alexis (17 at the time) remove the drain." I didn't know how Alexis would feel about doing that, but it shows how much I wanted to take control of the situation that was really scary and, to be honest, annoying.

How dare my body get cancer! I really didn't deserve that hardship one bit. I'm sure you've heard that denial is the first stage of grief. Anger is the second. I was well on my way to the third one: bargaining. Depression and acceptance, fourth and fifth on the list, would soon be on the emotional menu, although I was unaware of any of these stages at the time. I just put my head down and plowed forward with my life. Cancer wasn't going to get the better of me, no siree.

Actually, Florida was just the elixir I needed to start my healing. The five of us—me, Alexis, her friend Trine, Brittany, and her friend Rachel—had so much fun. The denial of my situation must have been so great that I forgot about those annoying stitches and worked overtime to ignore the pain.

But reality bit me hard when I pulled up to the parking garage. I yelped when I tried to insert the card into a machine with my left arm. Doing so was a stark reminder that I still had stitches holding in the drain. Small price to pay for all the fun we had. But mentally, I said, "Note to self: Think before using your left arm, PLEASE!" In my defense, I didn't have a choice because I had to insert the card in two different machines to get in and out of the parking garage.

Toward the end of the week, I thought it was time to remove the drain. Alexis had to cut some stitches and pull the drain. Yow! Did that hurt! She asked me if she should stop.

"Just get it out!" I said, in a not-so-friendly voice.

I regretted making my daughter perform surgery on me, but it had to be done. I thank her every day for her courage. Due to my impatience, the drain had to be reinserted two weeks after we returned because my underarm filled with fluid to the size of a grapefruit.

Chemo started on December 8, 2005, with surgery also that day to insert a port in my right chest. Ports are used so that chemo technicians don't have to puncture your skin each day to deliver the chemicals. They just inject the drug directly into the port. The first day of chemo I didn't feel too bad.

The second or third day was when it hit me. I got very nauseated and ached everywhere. I had to inject a drug into my stomach after each chemo to keep my red blood cell count up in case I got an infection. That drug made me ache like a bad flu. Of course, my friends who had had breast cancer warned me all this was coming. Up to now, it had all been an intellectual understanding.

Then, as they warned, my hair started falling out. Not just a few strands here and there but in clumps. There is no preparing a person for how shocking this side effect will feel. Each trip to the shower, each brushing, even just running my hands through my hair made me want to sob. My beautiful hair! Will it ever grow back? I wondered. Add to that list my eyebrows and eyelashes too. Whelp, no makeup for me for a while, I said, trying to look on the bright side.

I decided to go by myself to buy a wig. I watched in horror as the beautician shaved the rest of my hair off. Finally, it occurred to me: Sue, you have cancer. I picked out a wig that was close to my natural color of light brown. The cap onto which the "hair" was sewn felt funky on my bare skin, but I had been told that wearing a wig was for my mental health.

It wasn't one of the horribly expensive wigs, like the ones made of natural hair. I purchased a cheaper one made of synthetic "hair." I suppose I looked okay. At least I wasn't bald. And the wig kept my head warm. Heat leaves the body through a bald head. I left the store sporting my new wig and stood by my car for a while. I was unable to drive until I calmed down.

It was a typical December day: cold and very windy. Finally, I took myself in hand and decided to get on with things. My pity party had to be short-lived because I had kids and responsibilities. When tragedy strikes, I tend to go into action and avoid moping. My theory is that if I stay active, I am not reminded of my bad situation every minute of every day. In action, I have some control over my response. In a long pity party, I am giving in to my circumstances and making everyone around me feel my defeat. Telling myself that I *am* a strong person helps me believe I am strong. Knowing that my Father in heaven has a plan for me is comforting because I know I am not alone in my struggle. I know I am strong because I have triumphed over every adversity coming toward me. It hasn't been easy, but my faith gives me confidence. Nothing was going to change by my standing around feeling sorry for myself. So, I got out my keys, jumped in my car, and started the engine.

When I caught sight of myself in the review mirror, I screamed! The wig hair was sticking straight up. I looked like a Troll doll. The hair wasn't orange, but it still looked like a fright wig. After the wind had tousled the "hair," it hadn't fallen back down like my old hair would have. I smoothed it down, and finally realized the ridiculousness of how it looked. I laughed at how funny I looked. It's funnier looking back, but I was crying and laughing simultaneously at the time. (I am glad I could find some humor in cancer. I'll have to put that skill on my resume.)

In a sharp slap back to reality, I said to myself, "This is my life now. I have no control over this cancer." I took to heart the sentiment in the Serenity prayer: "...accept the things I cannot change..." The rest I leave for God.

In total, I ended up with many rounds of chemo and six weeks of radiation. One drug, Toxol, was so powerful it gave me permanent neuropathy in my toes and fingers. Neuropathy makes your extremities numb like they are asleep, accompanied by tingling and pain. At first, I couldn't have the covers over my toes at night. Now, it's a bit better. I now can stand the bed covers, but other consequences have appeared. Sometimes I won't be standing up. With numb toes, balance is a constant issue. My falls can happen very quickly and be extreme—31 stiches in my forehead from one tumble. My walking consists of the heel and ball of my foot with no toes involved in the process. For me, neuropathy is permanent after trying acupuncture and drugs with no improvement.

I had radiation every day for six weeks. In the waiting room, I and the other people who were there for radiation would talk each day. There were a number of us who were Christians. One couple was there with their daughter; the husband had had cancer the year before. They were from Alaska, so they traveled to Seattle for her treatment.

Toward the end of my treatment, the receptionist told me that the couple and their daughter had left for Alaska but had left a card they wanted to give me. It was a beautiful "stay strong" card, and inside was their grandmother's old lace handkerchief. In the card it said to use the handkerchief when all I could do was cry. Cancer really sucks, but you do meet some awesome people along the way.

Eventually the day came when I'd finally beaten the Beast. I was deliriously happy and went to work as always, traveled a lot more, and bought birthday presents for my grandkids.

Then, bam! Fifteen years later in 2020, the Beast returned for a second round—this time, Stage 4. This point is usually when your doctor tells you to get your affairs in order. You quickly realize your time on earth is on a countdown. And all this after I'd already had the works for cancer 15 years ago: surgery, radiation, and heavy-duty chemo in 2005. I had even thrown out my wig.

How unfair, I thought, that I had to duke it out with this monster a second time. But we cancer survivors make a strong bargain when we go into treatment: We get to live, but we must accept the brutal reality of medical issues that can arise in the aftermath of our treatment. They can last years after your treatment is done. Chemo is, after all, a poison that aims to kill the cancer cells, and radiation amounts to burning your flesh until you can't take anymore without more dire consequences. Nobody gets off scot-free without lingering side effects, with some of them being pretty annoying.

If I dwell on the consequences of cancer treatment, I remind myself that all of it is God's plan. Push on, Sue, I tell myself. Just put one foot in front of the other so you can enjoy the gift of another beautiful day. When I get down about cancer's return, I wonder how many people would love to have had this reprieve—two more years and counting to live the life that I adore now.

LIKE A THIEF IN THE NIGHT

How I was diagnosed a second time is a story in itself.

I had been to the shooting range that day. Even though I have a high tolerance to pain, I felt terrible afterward. My back hurt, my neck hurt, actually, *everything* on my body was registering mega-pain. Of course, I ignored it, as I usually do. I was just out of shape, I thought.

David (my "jackpot" husband you will read about later in Chapter 8) and I went golfing months before the shooting range. Lovely course, super weather in Arizona where we were escaping the doom and gloom of Seattle's rainy winter weather. Then without thinking about what I was doing, I got my finger stuck in the pushcart. It hurt like there was no tomorrow. I shouted, "Oh, that really hurts!"

David said, "Okay, Sue, does it really hurt?"

I replied, "That really f'ing hurt." Using that awful word was our way of determining whether it was just general grousing about a little boo-boo or to signal when I'm really in pain. "*It really f'ing hurts*!" I shouted. I trudged on, however.

In the middle of December, we went out for Mexican food. Very enjoyable, especially in Arizona. But I became terribly ill. Was it food poisoning? I didn't know, but it kept getting worse.

Food poisoning isn't something to fool around with, and because it persisted, we went to the ER on New Year's Eve. The ER doc ordered a CAT scan of my gut to see what was causing the symptoms. The scan revealed that something looked suspicious with my liver. Next stop, a liver biopsy.

The results of the biopsy were back. As my primary care

physician started talking, I sat down. (Good thing too.) "What did you say?" I asked him to repeat the diagnosis.

"You have tumors on your liver."

He told me to schedule an appointment with an oncologist for a further evaluation. That command didn't sound good at all.

I also complained about my neck and back hurting under my right shoulder, like *a lot*. He had me bend this way and that but said nothing further about it.

So, with dread in my heart, I dragged myself to the oncologist for some other tests.

My fears were confirmed. Dr. Singavi sat down, looked at me, and announced, "It's Stage 4 cancer. It's metastasized. This cancer is terminal, but we do have several cancer drugs we can try." He put a referral in for a PET scan to see where my body was affected. It was now in my lungs. And liver. And hips. And skull. I even had a broken rib because the cancer was in my bones now too.

The Beast had returned for a second bite of the apple. Oh, wait, there's more.

That backache I complained about? "Your back is actually broken," he said.

He explained that the cancer had eaten through the T4 (fourth thoracic) vertebra just above the shoulder blades. It had also eaten away my T9 joint below my shoulder blades, which was causing that hellacious pain.

So, yes, it *really, really, really f'ing hurt*!

I stumbled out of the building and into the parking lot where David was pacing. (He couldn't go in with me because of the COVID virus.) I fell into his arms and said, "I have cancer," and burst into tears. So did he. We held each other sobbing in the parking lot for a long time. We both felt dread, anticipating and not knowing what it would mean for our future. We were so much in love and only five years into our wonderful marriage. His first wife had died of cancer within two months of diagnosis. I'm sure David thought I would be gone in a few months.

If you have ever had a doctor deliver massively devastating news, you will understand when I say that I went blank after he said it was Stage 4. The rest was a blur. I couldn't even begin to absorb the totality of the results until some time had passed.

There would be no way to determine the action plan until I had more tests done. Ah, tests. We love our tests, don't we?

As a stopgap measure to ease my pain from the broken back, the doctor referred me to Cancer Care Alliance in Seattle and also to the University of Washington Medical School because I was going to be in Seattle for a visit. The plan was to inject cement into the vertebra to strengthen the bone and protect the nerves running down the spinal cord from exposure, which had been the job of all vertebrae. Sadly, the tumor had grown out of the bone, meaning cancer was too close to my spinal cord, meaning the treatment was not viable.

The docs are treating me with oral chemo this time. The side effects are much milder. I have a monthly bone infusion and shots to take the estrogen out of my body. I will be on chemo for the rest of my life.

I have some pretty bad days with almost unendurable pain, like at a 10—make that 11—but I'm doing pretty well so far. Statistically, this drug works on patients for 20 months, at which point it should be changed. When it stops working, doctors will put me on another one until that one stops working, then another and another until…you can fill in the rest.

The good news is that this drug has been working for 29 months, so I beat the odds with this one. Yay for me! That said, I need to have some lesions removed from my liver soon since they have cropped up lately.

I get a week off from the meds for my body to recover. Chemo makes you lose red blood cells, so the white cell count is higher. I get tired toward the end of the week off from the drug, Ibrance. I start bruising because my immune system isn't working all that well by that point. Now, I get my blood tested at least once a month, looking for markers indicating any changes in the disease.

Pain pills like acetaminophen and ibuprofen help somewhat. But when my pain becomes so overwhelming, they barely scratch the surface. I won't take opioids because of the horrible side effects. I won't lie: Day after day after day of being in all this pain and knowing it's not going to get any better wears on me. But I also know that Jesus is my 24-hour counselor. I pray about my situation and leave the problems with him. Still, I do believe there are such things as miracles. But I'm also okay with whatever the circumstances are.

TRUTH BE TOLD

I'm on the cancer train now, and the doctors are the engineers running it. They tell me when to get off one med and on another. I'm just along for the ride. I have no control over any of it. But I *do* have control over how I react to the situation.

With the time I have left, I want to help as many people as I can. I want to look at what I *can* do, not what I can't. I want to make memories with my kids and grandkids (we have 13 grands and 1 great on the way). I have so many people praying for me that I know God has me at the top of his list of children. To counteract any depression from the pain, I envision God in a big rocking chair with me in His arms. He is holding and comforting me.

If I ever need to look for consolation in all of this cancer stuff, it comes from my experience plowing through all of the drugs, scans, tests, infusions, and pain that has turned me into an expert on how to handle all of it. It has also sensitized me to others less fortunate than I am.

That experience, along with my high tolerance of pain, has

helped me weather lots of non-cancer-related situations. I have a pretty sunny disposition. Always have. I'm the second child of six in my family and the eldest of five girls. I am 10 years older than my youngest sister. I took care of her a lot, as often happens to older sisters in big families.

So, when that same sister got breast cancer after I did, I flew into action because I knew just what she was going through. Her reaction was typical of a lot of cancer patients: She stayed in bed, didn't go to work, and had no idea how to meet the moment with this diagnosis.

I just shepherded her through everything: the drugs, wig, food, scans, pain, fear, shock. If I hadn't done it myself, I wouldn't have had a clue what to do or how to make her laugh at the absurdity of it all. (She loved my story about the Troll wig.)

She is better now. But guess what? I have two *other* siblings diagnosed with breast cancer—and one of them is my brother. Yes, men get breast cancer too but at a dramatically lower rate. Fewer than 1% of all cases diagnosed are men. It's not genetic; we've looked into that possible cause.

Still, we wonder. We six siblings grew up under the flight path at SeaTac airport. Was that environment the cause of so much cancer among us? Airplanes roaring overhead hourly, if not more often, were irritating but not cancer-causing. How about the exhaust from the burnt jet fuel, which releases some petrochemicals? Again, no, most of that dissipates into the atmosphere. Or so I've read. One day we'll know.

CHAPTER 4

BETRAYAL AND DIVORCE

I often wondered if God was testing me in the years before I committed fully to Him in 1991 after my near-death experience during the birth of my daughter. Was He trying to get my attention by having some very unpleasant things happen to me?

The truth is that He does sometimes test us—dare I say, even shocks us. Indeed, one of those horrible shocks turned out to be my first marriage and divorce. So, yes, He gets our attention in such ways. Sadly at the time, I was distracted and wasn't listening.

BREAKING VOWS

Divorce is an ugly word, and it was a lot uglier when I was growing up. People used to stay married, *no matter what.* Even with abuse, neglect, or financial strain, they stayed in the relationship. The gist behind such perseverance was especially important for women because everyone *knew* that divorcées needed a husband to support them. That need meant they were regarded as constantly on the hunt for that one special man, that knight in shining armor who would whisk them off to live happily in a huge house with a pool and maids, and so on.

The problem for divorced women was that their status marked them as easy pickings for unscrupulous men who needed a wife to cook, clean, and fetch them a cold one after a hard day's work. And let's not forget about the bedroom...

Maltreatment aside, sticking it out through the hard times was a no-brainer for me, especially because I am loyal, loyal, loyal. It would never occur to me to bail on someone with whom I had taken a vow before God to cherish and obey until death. Beyond my own commitment, getting divorced would definitely invite looks of disapproval from my church community, as well as my family, because I obviously didn't have the fortitude to make the marriage work. So, I stuck it out as long as I could. Now I understand that divorce may be the only option for what ails a bad marriage.

Let me tell you this sad story.

I was an impressionable 19-year-old. I'd just graduated from high school in June 1972. Community college was my goal. I had been dating this guy, Bill, for a year and was very much in love with him.

One day, when we were still dating, he sat me down, looked me in the eye, and said quite seriously, "I have brain cancer."

I had no words to express my emotions. I felt sorry for him and wanted to help him through his crisis. Then he asked me to marry him. Of course, the brain cancer condition bothered me. How will I care for him? What will happen to me when he dies? Can I bear being around someone I love who is dying?

We got married anyway.

His story was complex with many details, but one thing would become clear: He exploited my kindness and commitment. Boy, did he spot me a mile away as a compassionate, true, trusting, helpful type.

But wait, there's more.

Bill was working a warehouse job, and I was at an office supply company. Six months after we married, he told me the cancer story was a lie.

I was devastated, betrayed, hurt. I had been so emotionally involved, worrying constantly about his illness and what I could do to help. Then to have him so off-handedly announce that he was dishonest…I had no way to deal with that duplicity and betrayal.

I cried and cried, not understanding that anyone could be so cruel. How could a person who supposedly loved me lie straight to my face and keep the lie going? I had to think he told this lie to trick me into marrying him. Red flag #1.

To make matters worse, he decided he didn't want to work

anymore. However, he liked to spend money and had grandiose ideas about how his life would progress. Red flag #2.

It's hard to explain the idea of someone like me, who thinks she is intelligent and strong, living under the control of another person. Things gradually got worse. I lost my self-esteem along the way. If I agreed with him and kept my mouth shut, I wouldn't have to listen to criticism and cross-examination.

I think I was disposed to this kind of go-along-to-get-along approach because I never saw my mom and dad quarrel in front of us kids. Mom just did what Dad said. She didn't contradict him ever. And they stayed married for 63 years until Dad's death. Consequently, we kids didn't learn how to have a healthy argument. As a result, I buried my opinions throughout my marriage. I'm not blaming them for my divorce, but I had a steep learning curve when it came to understanding how to stand up for myself.

Bill had colossally bad judgment too. He had a pilot's license to fly small planes by sight only. So, one weekend, he decided we should rent a plane to fly to Pullman, Washington, to see my brother and sister-in-law. After a fun weekend, Bill decided to fly back on Sunday. I told him the weather forecast did not look good. It was supposed to be cloudy and rainy—conditions that might cause problems with visibility enroute. He poo-poohed my doubts and announced he could make it home, no problem. I was very concerned, but again, I kept my mouth zipped. He was the one with the pilot's license. I was just his wife.

We started off the runway and flew up over the Cascade

mountains, where there was absolutely *no* visibility. Plus, the wings started icing. Not only does ice deform the shape of the wing and alter its aerodynamics, but it also adds weight to the aircraft that can affect its performance by reducing lift. Our little single-engine plane was bouncing all over because of the weather. I didn't need a pilot's license to know we were in trouble. I was petrified that we would crash. I hung onto the strap so I wouldn't go headlong into the windshield if we did. The turbulence nauseated me to no end.

In the first display of good judgment that day, he finally called the tower to tell them our situation. We both listened intently. I learned to monitor several instruments as the tower controllers talked us into the airport. We really couldn't see anything until just before landing.

You often hear about the need to kiss the ground after experiencing turbulence, and that's exactly what I did. I thanked God I don't know how many times for saving us. The FAA revoked Bill's pilot license for six months. Do you know how badly I wanted to say, "I told you so?" But admonishment wasn't going to happen. Not that day, not for a long time. You guessed it: Red flag #3.

When a person is in the middle of craziness, it is often hard to tell what is reasonable. I saw him engaging in so many things that lacked sound judgment. I mean, almost crashing a small plane due to bad weather over the mountains was one thing. As the months passed, I saw him engage in other activities that lacked good sense. Like smoking pot. Marijuana turned out to be a huge part of Bill's life. He even had a whole grow operation at home, which don't forget, was way before pot was legal anywhere in the states. Not to mention that if he got arrested, it would mean that I would also be thrown into the clink. My anxiety over being arrested was constant.

To divert my attention away from that fear, I threw myself into my job and set my sights on possibilities for advancement at Foster Office Equipment, the office supply business where I worked during high school and the first year of marriage with Bill. Two years to the date after I started the office supply job, I started a new job doing accounts payable at Safety and Supply Company. I worked hard to make enough money to pay for my husband's spending choices. Meanwhile, he found a rusted 1952 MG TD convertible in California. The car was shipped to Seattle on my dime. Shortly thereafter, packages began arriving from England with new MG parts. The crazy thing is that I believed I had no power over his spending. Red flag #4.

Things got even worse. Bill started controlling my comings and goings and limiting my contact with others. If I came home a few minutes late from work, he'd accuse me of being with another man. Clearly, I was in an emotionally abusive marriage. But my emotions kept me from seeing it.

At a certain point, I started feeling quite ill. I went to a doctor who diagnosed me with tonsillitis. I had two rounds of antibiotics. No change. When my tonsils were almost swollen shut, I went to a new doctor. A blood test was taken immediately that showed I had mononucleosis. My physician called me at work with the results. He ordered me to go home immediately and rest; otherwise, he said, I would wind up in the hospital.

I showed up at home in the middle of the day desperately wanting some chicken soup, Chamomile tea, and some good old-fashioned TLC. But instead of comforting me and putting me in bed, I got a verbal grilling from Bill about who had given me mononucleosis. He refused to help me as I convalesced. And such neglect was after I had been willing to take care of him when he supposedly had a brain tumor. (My mom ended up coming to take care of me.) By then, I was seeing red flag #5.

A few other episodes brought our union to an end. My husband came home with a Chevy El Camino purchased—again—on my dime without my knowledge. Then he came home one night drunk and high with another man in tow, and that recklessness was the last straw. Not only did Bill immediately go to the bedroom where he passed out, he left me with this strange man whom I did not know. It took a while to remove the stranger from our house.

When I went to my car to go to work in the morning, imagine my surprise when I discovered that man had been hanging around our house all night. He said my husband told him that I would give him a ride into the city. I was furious and did not offer the ride to this stranger. Bill had never even introduced me. (I'd lost count of the red flags at this point.)

That incident was *the* last straw. I'd reached my breaking point. When I got home from work, I kicked Bill out of the mobile home that *I* had purchased. After three years of this incredibly abusive and self-esteem-killing marriage, I demanded a divorce. Free at last and good riddance!

In typical self-centeredness, Bill thought we would eventually get back together. By this point, though, I was fed up with his lies, irresponsibility, and emotional abuse, so reuniting was a laughable joke on him. It took this long to realize I was not the crazy one and began standing up for my rights and demanding truth over lies. I was 22 years old and could support myself financially. We didn't have any kids together by his choice. I didn't have to be one of those frantic divorcées who needed a sugar daddy to survive.

As for living alone, solitude would be a far sight better than living with this creep. Frankly, people who say that divorce is a cop-out do not understand how destructive a person like Bill can be to another's physical and mental health.

FREEDOM OF CHOICE

I was the first in my family to divorce. Luckily, my parents were happy that I had extricated myself from that jerk, even though they had never said a bad word about our marriage. They could clearly see how I was being treated. Looking back, I ponder what would have happened if I had had a personal relationship with Christ at that time so I could have shared my thoughts and prayed for enlightenment over this horrible situation.

I wish I could say that I learned my lesson about attracting liars and cheaters. Why don't I have better judgment about these people? I kept wondering.

I concluded that I was very trusting of others because I was raised to always look at the good in people. Maybe I thought they should be trustworthy because I am trustworthy and loyal. I was taught that if I didn't have something nice to say, I shouldn't say anything. I never imagined there would be narcissists and outright liars like Bill, who have no empathy or sense of other people's needs. How can a person look you in the eyes and lie with no hint of guilt or remorse? How can a person keep a lie going, knowing they are torturing someone they supposedly love? My mind just doesn't work like that.

CHAPTER 5

SECOND MARRIAGE—AND DEATH

In choosing my second husband, I was extra mindful, and a little skittish, about committing to another man. After all, I could support myself, so I didn't *need* to get married. That fact alone helped me evaluate my next partner with a colder eye.

It had been two years since my divorce from the guy who almost killed me in an airplane. I had been working at a very challenging job at the Safety and Supply Company since age 19. I had replaced a woman named Irene, who left to take care of her family. I didn't know squat about the business and even less about accounts payable. I think I was hired because my birthdate was the day before the office manager's birthday and she liked me.

The company stocked about 10,000 products. So my job was very busy. At first, the work was overwhelming, but it was the classic on-the-job training. True to my nature, I put my head down and just worked like a beaver until I got up to speed.

Jon, the son of the owner, ran a department dedicated to sales of various products and contracts for the Department of Defense. Jon sometimes would be on the phone with a customer and yell over, asking me where we purchased such and such product. When I didn't know the answer, he would say snidely, "Well, Irene would know." After several of these comments, I devised a card system where I would catalog the odd purchases so I could answer right away.

Some days were like living a sitcom mixed with real work. Back then, my work was done on a 36-inch-wide machine with keys all the way across. I would key in the date, invoice number, amount, and due date. Once I hit the enter key, the large carriage moved quickly to the right and then left again. Imagine my embarrassment when Sam, the owner, was at the file cabinets one day when I hit the enter button. The cartridge zoomed right and hit him square on the butt. Luckily, he thought it was pretty funny.

Other times, I felt like I was on an episode of *I Love Lucy* with all its hilarious scenarios. On one occasion, the mail arrived via a big canvas bag with ropes and a metal hook to close it. I was busy with other things, so I put it on the floor for a time when I could get to the mail. I had long hair at the time. When it was time to open the mail, I leaned over and pulled quickly on the metal clasp. I was too quick for my own good.

A big chunk of my hair caught in the clasp. I couldn't raise my head up, so I was trapped below my desk. I started calling out to my coworker, Wendy. I could see her looking around, but she couldn't see me and couldn't imagine where I was calling from.

Finally, she came around and started laughing. Wendy ended up pulling strands of hair out of the clasp to extricate me.

Then there was the time I fell over when I tried to walk away from my desk because a staple had hooked to both sides of my pantyhose at the knees. It's always an adventure with me.

In spite of my klutziness, I was promoted again because of the departure of the office manager. Would I take over that position? Sam asked. Well, here I went again, moving into a job I knew absolutely nothing about.

The work was true on-the-job training. Suddenly, I was working with attorneys, CPAs, insurance companies, payroll, and all employee benefits. Sam was no help because he had cancer and would sometimes be out of the office, which meant I was on my own when making decisions and handling employee issues.

This juncture was when Jon and I locked horns. Jon was supposed to calculate the monthly bonuses for all the outside salespersons. I needed the information by a certain time to input to ADP, one of the top payroll-processing companies we used to produce the payroll checks and reports. The deadline came and went with a deafening silence from Jon.

I was fuming. His tardy report meant I had to hand-type all the bonus checks. Mad is not a strong enough word to describe how I felt. Later, Jon said he was sorry and told me he owed me lunch. We had a pleasant conversation over burgers and fries, and eventually my anger cooled when I saw a different side of him. He must have felt the same attraction and asked me to dinner.

We dated without anyone at the office knowing. He impressed me because he worked hard and paid his bills on time. (A charming contrast from Bill's couch-potato act and careless attitude.)

Anyway, Jon and I were married on August 18, 1979. He had two kids, a 14-year-old boy named Shawn and an 11-year-old girl named Dionne. Shawn moved in with us the day we were married. Dionne lived in Spokane and moved in with us the following year.

Instant momhood! And to a teenage boy and tween girl. Again, a job I was put in charge of and about which I knew nothing. What could go wrong?

I had been working for the company for six years when we got married. Sam had already passed away. Sam had had a 50/50 partner that Jon inherited. I knew the partner because he would come into the office a couple of times a year and wanted me to serve him coffee. I wanted to tell him, "Get it yourself, Bub!" I also knew his skeletons in the closet, like his girlfriend whose apartment we paid for. The man was married. And society has the gall to accuse divorced woman of having bad morals.

Jon ended up buying out the partner with money and merchandise. Before the buyout, the partner made it clear he didn't trust me (probably because I knew too much about his sordid life...I think he needed to look in the mirror). I wanted to get out of that toxic situation, so I left to start my own business. I figured, why not?

I knew a lot about payroll, office management, deliverables, etc. All I needed was a product that would have mass appeal. So, I bought some radio frequency (RF) sealing equipment from a friend in Reno with which to manufacture certain kinds of tags for industry and for vinyl products whose seams could be sealed (think of how beach balls are sealed at the seams). The equipment was moved to Seattle and—*voilà!* —my new business, Vinatronics, was born. (Actually, the company was already named Vinatronics because the previous owner was Jim Vines, and the product was made with vinyl.)

With the RF equipment, we made black vinyl corner covers for the vendor who had the NFL contract for all desk calendars. Eventually we added sewing capability for road worker safety vests, a bag that held burn first-aid supplies for all Starbucks stores, and for other specialties.

DOUBLE DUTY

When I started my company, a new person who took over my duties at Jon's company was eventually fired. So, I ended up doing the books, payroll, and office management of *both* companies. My duties also included selecting and implementing all computer equipment. I didn't have small children at the time, so I worked 60-hour weeks. Actually, that may be a low estimate, now that I think about it.

Other challenges came along too. Early in our marriage, I realized Jon was an alcoholic. He would often show up at work drunk as a skunk. Everyone there knew he had a drinking problem, except me. I was raised in a family with no drinking so didn't have a clue about alcoholism. The upshot: I had to make decisions that he should have been making. I was exhausted.

Being my typically naive self, I thought I could change this predicament. After all, at least he wasn't growing pot or shaming me every minute of the day. That trade-off didn't mean it was easy, though. Many occasions were ruined because of his drinking.

Probably seven years into our marriage, I sought help from Al Anon, where I learned I had no control over another person's addiction. The truth is that only the individual can decide not to go down the horrible addiction path, but it takes strength and determination, neither of which he had. Despite my pleading, crying, and magical thinking that he could change if he loved me, nothing changed. I often made excuses for his drinking when we were with others. Stop doing that, Al Anon scolded, because when you cover for someone's addictive behavior, you are enabling the addict. That advice was an important lesson for me. I decided I was not willing to go down the addiction path with Jon. When I started looking for my own apartment, Jon entered a monthlong recovery program. His issues were more than alcohol. His past included being adopted at 18 months and being abused by his mother. It was clear he had never dealt with his abandonment issues.

Still, providence had prevailed in that Jon and I had tried to start our own family during our early marriage, with no luck. Now I see that God prevented that outcome until Jon was sober.

Once Jon quit drinking, we attended couples therapy to reset our relationship. I needed to trust him to stay sober and be a dependable, equal partner. That condition was nonnegotiable. I had overseen everything for those eight, long years and was exhausted. (Sound familiar?)

Then, with him in control of his life, our life was fabulous: Our businesses were flourishing, both my stepkids were happy, and best of all, Jon was completely sober. Jon and I worked well together in our businesses and rarely fought about anything.

The biggest fight we had was over fudge-covered Oreos. All day at work one day I had been thinking about having a fudge-covered Oreo when I got home. I went into the kitchen to discover Jon had eaten the whole package. Every single cookie was GONE. My anger was explosive. I soon realized that the cookies were not the problem but rather that he didn't consider me at all when he reached for that last cookie. It's true that we must pick our battles, but I was no longer willing to be subject to indifference by others. For years afterward, his apology was to gift me a box of fudge-covered Oreos on my birthday and at Christmas.

Our life together kept getting better and reached new heights. In 1987 we were blessed with our first child, Jarrod. In 1988 we were blessed with Alexis. In 1991 we had our miracle baby, Brittany. Jon was sober, and we had a good rhythm going with work and kids. Our life was full of family outings to the zoo, the state fair, and the children's museum.

We continued on our path of happiness and grew in new ways together as a family. When Jarrod turned eight, he weighed just enough to join the Little League football team, and Jon loved watching football. Jon, who was out of town at the time, told me to stop by Chubby and Tubby (a store packed to the brim with all kinds of merchandise) to get Jarrod a cup for his first football practice. Picture me in a hurry, wearing a work suit, in high heels, rushing down the aisle with three kids following behind. I picked up the cup and ran home to have Jarrod change just in time to make the practice.

On the first day of practice, Jarrod had trouble running down the field. The next day I asked another mother if her son had trouble running with the cup on. She looked at me and said, "What size did you buy?" I turned red and said, "I didn't know they came in sizes." My poor son of eight years old, barely weighing enough to make the team, was wearing a man's size XL cup. I felt so bad that my mistake caused him that pain!

Other solutions weren't as simple. Anyone with young kids knows that three kids with an odd man out are a challenge on any day. Brittany was often left out of a lot because she was three years younger than Alexis, and so if Jarrod and Alexis were playing a game and didn't want Brittany to play, Brittany grabbed pieces of the game and ran off. On other occasions, Alexis and Brittany played together with dolls and created what I thought was a pretend business, which they called Safety & Supply Company. One day, though, I discovered they were taking items out of the house and trying to sell them to the neighbors! Alexis had even made business cards that said KIDS CAN WORK in bold letters. Alexis is now a CPA...not surprising in that she would help me by entering figures into the computer with great accuracy at a very young age.

A SORROW WORSE THAN CANCER

All of our special times came to a screeching halt, however, on Saturday, April 15, 2000. Nearly 21 years after we were married, my life changed forever.

Jon and Shawn, who had gotten married years before, were at a meeting in Orlando, Florida. I had been at work that morning. When I arrived home, my daughter-in-law came running across my lawn with a horrible look on her face. She got into my car and told me Jon had died.

My reaction was, "What? No. What?!"

She related that the meeting had just ended after a week, and Jon and Shawn were in the hotel room having dinner when Jon started slurring his words and then fell to the floor. He was not responsive. Shawn called 911. The EMTs worked on him for a while in the room then took him immediately to the ER. But it was too late. He had already died of a heart attack made worse because of COPD (chronic obstructive pulmonary disorder) from smoking.

Shawn followed the ambulance to the hospital, and police took him aside and started questioning him. In Orlando, when someone dies in a hotel room, they consider it a homicide until they know otherwise. Shawn was beside himself with grief on top of incredulity that he was a suspect. They moved their belongings from the original room to another. By the time I found out Jon had died, it was hours after the event. I called airline companies to see about having his body shipped home, but the $10,000 fee was prohibitive. Since Shawn was in Orlando, he had the grim task of arranging to have Jon cremated there.

I couldn't sleep for days and did a lot of vacuuming. We planned a funeral for April 22, 2000. There were around 300 people who came to the service. I had planned food for 75 at our residence. I called the local caterer, Husky Deli, and they came within 30 minutes with a lot more food. Grateful is not a strong enough word for Jack Miller and his staff.

I was dazed. Grief does that. Jon was only 53. I thought we would have another 30 years together. I tried to get his remains sent in time for the funeral. It turned out that FedEx or any other fast carrier would not take them. So, my husband's remains ended up coming home via U.S. Postal Service. The postal carriers' motto is "Neither snow nor rain nor heat nor gloom of night stays these couriers from the swift completion of their appointed rounds." But they weren't so swift on this occasion. His remains didn't arrive in time for his funeral. The day after his funeral was Easter and my birthday. Now I was a 46-year-old divorced, widowed woman.

After Jon died, I would wake up at 4:30 a.m. every day. That was the time Jon had left for his trip to Orlando. As usual, Jon always picked out his clothes, and I packed his suitcase. I had no idea that was the last time I would see him.

No one could have explained to me how it feels to lose a spouse. I felt like I had a brick inside of me that hurt so much. The feeling didn't go away. In fact, things got worse. I started having panic attacks and couldn't breathe. Brittany was 8 years old when Jon died, Alexis was 11, and Jarrod was 13. Shawn and Dionne were in their 30s.

Shawn brought Jon's suitcase back with him. It was very difficult for me to open it. I could smell his cologne and cried. There was a chain he wore that I kept by my bedside. I would smell it every night. I missed Jon being with me in bed. The fact that I could never ask him another question about our businesses or how to raise the kids was daunting. My heart was shattered.

After losing a spouse, I completely lost myself. The world keeps on spinning, and other people go about their daily lives, but your life stops abruptly. I was just wandering in a fog. When a spouse dies you go from being a wife to nothing. The widowhood club is not one I wanted to join.

For a long period of time, I was lost trying to figure out where and how I fit back into the revolving, fast-paced world. Dealing with my kids' grief was also very hard. We often wished Dad were there for moments like graduations and weddings. During this time, I sometimes felt like just pulling the covers over my head forever. Lying in bed in the quiet by myself was very hard, and I would cry many nights, missing my husband.

Grief takes a lot of time and patience to heal. Even something as mundane as going to the dry cleaners was a painful stab in my heart when they asked me why Jon hadn't picked up his clothes. In another instance, I had gone to Macy's and happened to find some swim trunks Jon had been looking for. I was so excited until I got to the register and realized he wouldn't need them. I stood there holding the trunks just bawling. The clerk didn't know what to do. I set them down and ran out of the store.

Every holiday, birthday, and anniversary was different after Jon died. Jon loved Christmas so much. He used to take time picking out the perfect gift for all of us. He would be up and showered at 5 a.m. on Christmas morning drinking coffee with the video recorder in his hand. Every 15 minutes, he would ask if he could wake up the kids. My answer was always no. The kids got up early anyway because they were so excited to see that Santa had come to their house. One Christmas Eve, Jarrod opened the fireplace insert to solve the mystery of how such an old fat man got in and out. I was in the kitchen when he reported that there was no way Santa could come through the fireplace insert. Jarrod was our question child. There was no handle on the inside to open it, he declared, plus it was way too small, he added. I told him it was magic. Right about that time, we watched the movie *The Santa Clause* with Tim Allen. Then Jarrod said he understood how Santa did it. Kids are great, especially at Christmas.

One of my go-to coping mechanisms was to stay active. So, in the latter part of April, the kids and I took a trip to Sun River in Oregon. We skied in the morning and had other adventures in the afternoon. My three little kids learned how to snowboard at Mt. Bachelor.

One afternoon, I decided we should get a raft and go down the Deschutes River. When we got to the rental place, they only had canoes. We took a canoe, even though I had never been in one in my life. Jarrod thought he was a master canoer, so he and Alexis started paddling. Paddler alert! They couldn't coordinate their oars very well, so we ended up going backward, slammed into the bank, turned the canoe around, and started again.

I suggested they coordinate their paddles, to which Jarrod protested, "I do so know what I'm doing!" Things got heated enough that I told Jarrod to pull over to the bank. I told him to get out and walk back. Alexis and I had just started off when I heard a loud "Mom!" I turned around to see I had dropped Jarrod on an island. There was no chance of his walking back.

Alexis and I spent some real energy paddling upstream to rescue him, and we had a good laugh about it. The rest of the trip was wonderful with horseback riding, bike riding, and exploring Bend, Oregon. The trip was a distraction, but I missed Jon fiercely.

Upon our return home, I sought solace in my prayers to God and Bible study. It was comforting to come back to something so familiar and dependable as my religion. God understood the ache in my heart. I had to lean on Him a lot during the years after Jon's death. One day I threw myself on my bedroom floor and sobbed, asking God for help. I felt as though I were drowning. Shortly after that day, I felt I would be able to handle any circumstance as long as I just put one foot in front of the other and kept moving forward with God by my side. I felt that God could be my strength.

CHAPTER 6

THIRD MARRIAGE—TO THE CON

In November 2000, seven months after Jon's death, a man whose kids also attended my kids' school called out of the blue and asked me to go for coffee. I'll call him The Con because I don't want to use his real name. I'd seen him around but didn't know him.

He asked me a lot of questions as we sipped our lattes but didn't tell me much about himself. We got together some more times and went to the movies and a play. We had only been dating for two weeks when he told me he loved me. I didn't know what to make of his hasty advances. He seemed to morph into everything I would be looking for in a partner.

Right there is where my antennae should have gone up. But seven months is hardly long enough to mend my heart that had been shredded from Jon's sudden death and the end of our long, loving marriage. My eyes were still clouded from heartache. Not to be deterred, The Con pushed so hard to get married. (Again, with the red flags!)

I had become pretty shrewd in my old age (about time!) and had him sign a prenuptial agreement, which he didn't want, and married him in June 2001. We now had a blended family, with his two kids at my house three days a week. Man, was I in for some surprises!

It turned out The Con had lied to me about his previous marriage. (Later, I found out that there were a lot more.) He didn't want me to contact his ex-wife. Then there was the isolation from my family and friends. Our time alone and with the family had to revolve around him. It's a typical move by someone who wants to dominate your life, just like my first husband had. That way, all your support groups and ways of bouncing ideas off them were cut off.

Soon, I was in a nightmare. The Con had a job and made good money but would not pay for anything, including food. He said that because my house was in my name only, he wouldn't contribute anything to the household including food for his children. The Con turned out to be very narcissistic and had obsessive-compulsive disorder (OCD) from what I could tell. He had many lotions and potions that he used every day. He had a precise order in which he had to use these. When he fixed his hair, he would hit the brush hard on the sink exactly eight times. I was afraid the porcelain was going to break. When The Con came home from a trip, he would spend at least an hour rearranging household items to the exact spot he decided they should stay. One time, I moved many things around so I could watch him do the rearranging and know I was not crazy. Everything we did revolved around what he needed and wanted. I found out that he didn't have auto insurance, so I also paid for that for my and my kids' sake.

On top of all that, something very weird happened after we were married. He wanted me to have breast implants, but I had to pay for it. I told him absolutely not. I told him to pay for a penile implant on himself and then I would consider it. Two can play this game, I thought.

After five months of marriage and dealing with his OCD, I decided to surprise him for his birthday. He was working in Arizona at the time. He told me the hotel had a shuttle from the Phoenix airport that he would take each time. I arranged for someone to take care of all the children, got on a plane, and headed to Arizona.

I called the hotel to tell them I needed a ride because I was surprising my husband. No one arrived after some time. So, I called once more. Still, no one came, so I called a third time. Finally, a van showed up. When I got in, the driver told me that The Con had to get rid of the girlfriend before he could come get me. I repeated his words to The Con, but he just said the driver must have been joking.

Is he joking? I thought. That's how naive I was.

He wasn't joking.

When I got home, I turned on The Con's computer on the desk. Imagine my horror when I saw all manner of porn spewing out of it. I looked in his email and could see he was corresponding with call girls and asking their rates. Imagine my shock and disbelief, hurt and disgust. When he got home, I confronted him with the evidence.

He did not confess. Instead, he told me I was crazy. (That's called gaslighting and is typical behavior with narcissists.) He had no empathy or remorse. It was like he was void of emotion unless it was for himself. Why did I keep attracting these toxic men? My mistake was in trusting someone I didn't know very well. Strength was not part of my mental state when he approached me and pushed to get married. The Con was very practiced at making himself morph into what a woman thinks she needs. I cried. I realized he didn't care that he was hurting me. At that point, I was convinced I may be in trouble but wasn't sure what to do. I started praying, something I should have done well before I agreed to marry.

Six months after we married, I refinanced my house. I didn't put him on the mortgage because it was my house and part of the prenup. The Con was upset and threw a fit. He said he couldn't love me because the prenup was coming between us. He decided we needed to go to counseling with a Christian counselor. That answer was fine with me. He found the counselor.

Our conversations in counseling always came back to the prenup and how I needed to cancel it. Finally, the counselor told him directly that I was not canceling the prenup. Then The Con ginned up some cockamamy story about how I had taken $165,000 of his money.

"What have you done with it?" he shouted.

By this time, the counselor had caught on to The Con's tricks and asked him to bring in a complete accounting of what he claimed he was owed. Well, The Con picked the wrong person to bamboozle. I had down to the penny what he spent and could account for all his money. I foresightedly never had a joint account with him. After a few more counseling sessions, I told The Con and the counselor I was filing for divorce.

That's when The Con sprang into action. He hired a female attorney but failed to tell her I was his seventh marriage. He played like he knew nothing about divorce. He told his attorney that he had to stay at my house until his renters were out of his. That was a lie because he was working on buying a house up the hill from me. It took two years from the point of our marriage to finalize the divorce and remove him from my home. The Con told me straight out that he wanted property or money. That wasn't going to happen.

The months that The Con lived with us until the divorce was final were scary. One day, as he was shouting at me and threatening me, Jarrod came running upstairs with a baseball bat to protect me. But I had already discovered that if I started the video recorder, The Con would stop being abusive. I put locks on all the bedroom doors except the one The Con was living in. I took my kids and left the house for a vacation with all the doors locked just to get away for a short period. My attorney said The Con would be allowed time to get the renters out of his house. Depression and anger set in for me. Looking back, I should have insisted on getting a restraining order and making him leave my house. I felt so defeated and sick to my stomach. I think I was at my lowest point ever in dealing with this second narcissist. My plan was to get through the divorce and never trust again.

To be in the middle of divorce so soon after our marriage was embarrassing for me. Instead of having a very small wedding, The Con insisted on a big affair, consisting mostly of my friends. He really didn't have any friends, so some work acquaintances stood up for him. The Con also insisted on picking all the music, which consisted of songs by a group called Lone Star. In fact, all details for the wedding were planned by his insistence of what he wanted. Love is a funny emotion in that it can make a person not see the reality of the possible future. I should have realized that controlling behavior was a hugely important signal.

I did find out he was already pursuing a gal who worked at our local coffee shop and whose husband had just died of a brain tumor. Now I realized what his schtick was—go after widows who don't know which way is up and bilk them out of their money and house. But I got away from his clutches just in time. Maybe I was wising up after all.

The day that The Con moved out of my house, he brought a coworker to watch me to make sure I didn't steal from him. Of course, I caught them trying to move furniture that belonged to me. Our divorce was final in 2003.

That finale was my "Come to Jesus" moment. I really had to evaluate myself and why this mess happened. Looking back, I believe my logical mind was still compromised from losing Jon, making me much easier to manipulate.

They say you shouldn't do ANYTHING for a year after a spouse dies. Your mind is just too messed up, and that mindset includes being less able to assess relationships. I recommend—*plead* with—anyone reading this book to follow that advice. It could save you a whole lot of trouble.

Me, Shawn Holding Jarrod, Jon, Dionne

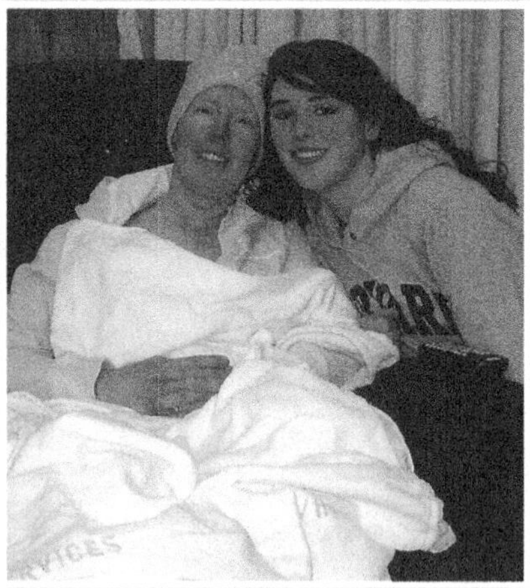

Me and Brittany—Doing Chemo

Jarrod Football Practice

My Birth Family

Me and David

Francis with Beau in the nursing home.

My Dad and my Mom

Me with the drain that Alexis removed

Brittany, Olivia, Alexis

Me, Jarrod, Colleen, David

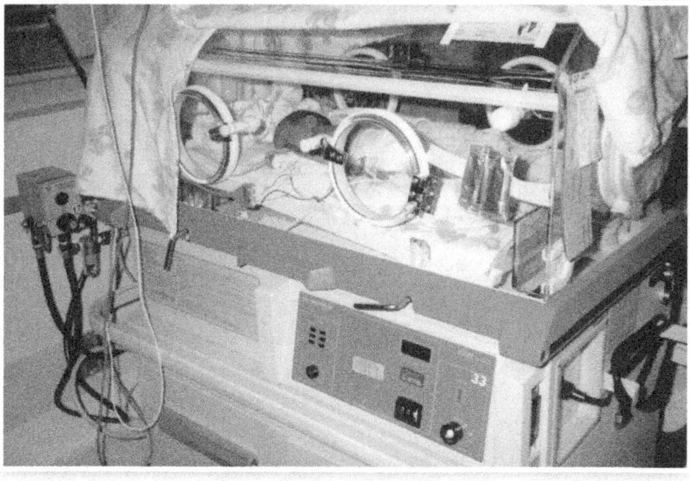

Brittany in the incubator

My late son Shawn with Olivia

Jarrod, Olivia, Colleen

Jill, Colleen, David

Brittany, Alexis, me, Jarrod on my College Graduation at 53

Christer, Ethan, Liam, Christi, Ellie

Alexis, Jarrod, Brittany, Shawn, Dionne

My Dad's internment with someone else's beautiful Flowers

CHAPTER 7

DEMENTIA

Fortunately, tragedy usually comes in decently spaced intervals, although that timing is never comforting. For me, it reappeared when Dad developed dementia later in life. That disease does funny things to people's memories, and sufferers can often become uninhibited when dealing with emotions.

At first it showed up as a little forgetfulness or not knowing how to use something. Dad did all repairs on the house and car, as well as taking care of the finances. He was an engineer, so he was very detail oriented. Mom noticed something wasn't right before any of us kids saw it.

One year after Dad completed their taxes, the IRS sent a letter saying the tax return had errors. Dad was very frustrated and asked me to look at the return. I found his errors and did a correction to the tax return. I asked Dad if I could just take over doing their taxes. My very strong, capable Dad started crying during our conversation. I felt horrible watching Dad cry.

The signs of his illness weren't as serious early on. Playing cards, for example, was an afternoon event for Dad and Mom. Uno and Skip-Bo were two favorites. Dad frequently forgot how to play, which made it difficult for Mom. But he still wanted to play cards, so my mom would sit with him every day trying to play along even though it didn't make sense.

He also was always very proud to have served in World War II in the South Pacific. But whenever we asked him about his war experience, he clammed up—that is, until he developed dementia. Soon, he began recounting horrific tales of having to shoot people during his tour. It made me sad that he had held those emotions inside most of his adult life. I was glad he could unburden himself.

In another example, a lack of inhibition occurred toward the end of his life. Dad had fallen into a coma. He had super care because every day he had one special nurse and helper turn him so he wouldn't get bed sores. One day, my dad came out of his coma, looked at the helper, and said very clearly, "She's got big knockers!" Dad quickly went back into the coma. The nurse doubled over with laughter and told us that made her whole week. My dad would never have talked like that in his pre-dementia days!

As the disease progressed, it got harder and harder for my mom. Dad wouldn't use the full tank of oil to heat the house. Instead, he set up electric heaters around the house. Mom would sit in her chair with an electric throw, gloves, and a hat to keep warm. Again, no logic involved.

One day, my mom called me in a panic asking me to come

quick. I was four houses away, so my son Jarrod and I ran over. Dad was trying to have my 5'3" mom hold a 4'x8' sheet of plaster board above her head so he could fasten it to the garage wall. Jarrod and I took over the project with Dad until he was finished.

Another horrifying day was when Dad was cutting drift-wood on the beach. He would have my mom hold the log as he cut it with the chain saw. The saw kicked off the wood and hit my mom in the mouth, knocking out a few front teeth. Instead of calling 911, he dragged her off the beach and took her to the emergency room. She ended up having plastic surgery and dental work to fix the damage. With that incident, my siblings and I were adamant that he must not use a chain saw again. We took the blade part away, but he later bought a new one. We took the whole chainsaw away and told him we would help him cut wood when he wanted.

Six of us kids would email periodically to update on the progress of the disease. The first happening was when my dad went into a rage because I wouldn't let him put a nasty letter into all the neighbor's mailboxes. It got so bad that I called 911 as he was throwing objects at my mom. The fire department came, but my dad would not cooperate. So they called the police.

Two large policemen came and told Dad he would be going to the hospital for evaluation. Dad stood up with his fists out to fight the police. The policemen had to handcuff my dad and strap him to a stretcher. All the while he was screaming at me and my sister, "Look what you've done to me!"

At Harborview, the main trauma hospital in Seattle, he was throwing trays at the nurses, so they had to tie him to the bed. The Senior Care doctors there are fantastic. Dr. May Reed took him off all his meds, discovered he had a bad urinary tract infection (UTI), which can cause rages, and started him back slowly on only medications they deemed necessary.

Before then, my dad used to take all his prescription meds out of the prescription bottles and put them in old film canisters, so we didn't know what he was taking. When the doctor would take him off a medication, he would keep taking it until it was gone because he had paid for it even though it may interfere with current meds.

Dementia not only has no cure but also is a progressive disease that is stressful on all involved and compounds otherwise ordinary chores. Let me recount the saga of my sister who had taken on the task of taking my folks to the bank and grocery store weekly. Dad and Mom would sit in the back seat of the car. At the bank, he would insist she drive him to the drive-through to put money in the bank and then circle around to the other side of the drive-through to take money out. Then he would go *into* the bank to check the balance. It could not be done in one transaction.

That oddity was minor compared to other events. Before the doctors discovered my dad's UTI, my sister was doing the bank run using her new car (her first ever new car). She started driving away from the bank, heard something, looked in the back and saw my dad trying to pee in a bottle, but it was going all over her new car's carpeting. She called me after this trip just furious. I told her Dad would pay for a detail job on her new car. That week our email subject was "Rolling Outhouses."

The problems continued. My dad tried to drive even though he had glaucoma and couldn't see well. My mom has macular degeneration, but my dad would use her to tell him if he was too far left or right in the lane. He also started getting lost on regular routes. I was the one who had to talk to him and take the car keys. He knew I had parked his car at my office but called the police anyway to report it stolen. When the police showed up at my office, I explained the situation.

Then I found out my dad was taking extra cash out of the bank to buy a new car. He also sent an appeal into the state asking to take a driver's test to get his license back. He studied and studied and passed the written test by one point. An appointment was scheduled to take the driving test. I happened to be out of town, so my sister took him.

There was a light out on the car, so the examiner told him he could not take the test. As the examiner was talking to him, Dad kept revving the engine loudly. The examiner told him to turn the engine off, but he wouldn't. Finally, my dad realized he couldn't take the test. He rescheduled.

For that new appointment, I was home. He hadn't driven in about five months, so he wanted to practice before taking the test. I told him to just drive up the hill and back down. But he kept going onto other streets. I was scared to death as he was all over the road. I got him to stop, and I drove us to the DMV.

At the DMV, I got into the front passenger seat to wait for the road test to start. Dad got in the driver's seat. He quickly turned the key, shoved the car into drive, and squealed out of the parking space into the parking lot. I reached over and was trying to remove the keys, saying no! He shoved the car into reverse and floored the gas. My mom was also in the back seat and neither of us was buckled in. We hit the parking curb, went airborne, and hit the building. We were stunned.

I got the keys out of the ignition, went into the DMV, and told them what happened. The supervisor said, "Well he can't take the test today because he had an accident, but he can reschedule."

I was dumbfounded. I screamed at the supervisor that my dad shouldn't be allowed to drive. The examiner who was present the first time that my dad tried to take the test was standing there and said, "I'm not ever getting in the car with him."

The supervisor came out to the car to talk to my dad. Dad told him the reason for the accident was because I was trying to take the keys out of the car. The supervisor asked Dad about all the dings on the car. "No big deal," Dad said, "just little bumps." Dad was told he would need a doctor's permission to take the test again. Luckily, I was taking him to a doctor appointment later that day. I called the doctor's office and told them that if they signed the form, any accident would be on them. They wouldn't sign, and my dad resigned himself to not driving anymore. The email subject line was "Crash Dummies."

Not long after that incident, my dad was admitted to the

hospital when we found out his UTI had gotten worse after antibiotics. On the drive to the doctor's office, Dad told me he felt like his body was shutting down. He went into a coma a few days after admission.

Dad passed away on May 20, 2013. Just a couple of hours before passing, he came out of a coma and said goodbye to us and the grandchildren. His send-off was good for my kids because they didn't really have closure when their dad died.

My dad was laid to rest at a beautiful military cemetery in Covington, Washington. My brother Paul crafted a box out of wood for Dad's ashes. Before internment, we kids and Mom decided to put some items in the box that reminded us of Dad. First was a bottle of correction fluid because he had started marking buttons on the television remote with it because he couldn't see which buttons were which. A secondary problem came when he couldn't remember which button did what even with the correction fluid. On top of that issue, he would call me to try and fix the TV, which was challenging because I couldn't see the button label under the correction fluid. The next item was a Christmas bow. Every Christmas he would attach a bow to his forehead like he was a present. The grandkids loved grandpa and his bow. Third was an emery board because he had them all over the house in case he got a hangnail.

Filling the box was an emotional but fun time remembering Dad. We also were happy when we went to the cemetery to put his box in the crypt because someone else had already been there and left fresh beautiful flowers when they laid their loved one to rest.

We laughed because Dad would never have approved of spending that much money on flowers.

My mom is now 93 and will be put in the same crypt when it is her time.

CHAPTER 8

FOURTH MARRIAGE—JACKPOT!

In terms of marriage, the fourth time was the charm for me. After so many disappointing and tragic experiences with husbands, I was beginning to think I was crazy. How could my judgment be so far off?

I was understandably gun-shy and leery about all men. Both Bill (first husband) and The Con (my third) had done me dirty. Obviously, my radar for detecting unscrupulous men was on the fritz. After dating too many frogs over the next 11 years, I begged off looking for my Prince Charming for four years.

I prayed a lot during this time. "God, you know me inside and out. You know everything about me. You know I don't want to be alone the rest of my life. If you have someone who fits me, please bring him to me, as I am done looking."

ANSWER TO A PRAYER

He must have been listening. He answered my prayer, but the story about how I met my fourth, current, and last husband is as complicated as a labyrinth. Here's the maze: My son, Jarrod, had a girlfriend. Eventually he found out she was married. So when they broke up, she revealed she was pregnant. Since she was married, her husband had to do a denial of parenthood through the court. To do this, DNA samples had to be taken from the baby and Jarrod to confirm the baby was Jarrod's. She was.

We met his darling little daughter, Olivia, a week before her first birthday. We asked her mom if we could see her on the birthday. Olivia's mom brought her to my house since Jarrod had moved back in with me. She left Olivia with us. Jarrod eventually got custody of Olivia since her mother just up and disappeared for periods of time and was not in a stable relationship. What a great dad he was! He set up a crib in his room and dove into parenthood. That little girl has brought so much joy to our family.

Wait, you're thinking: What the heck does this have to do with your new husband?

(I told you this was complicated. You'll love the ending.)

When Olivia was three, Jarrod started dating Colleen, who had moved to Seattle from Colorado. When they got married at my house, her parents were among the guests: David, her father, and Jill, her mother.

David, Jill, their younger daughter Christi and family, and

I became good friends. Every event or holiday was at my house. We would also go to dinner when they came to Seattle, which was often as both their daughters lived in Seattle. Christi was starting her own family. Colleen had moved to Seattle to be near her sister.

After Christi had her second child, David and Jill drove back to Colorado. Then the bad news hit: Jill had bladder cancer. She died two months after the diagnosis on June 7, 2013. David was completely upside down. He would call me when he was having a hard day. Being somewhat of an expert on grief, I told him he would eventually find a new normal.

David found a girlfriend after a time. They dated for about six to nine months before he realized she was not the one. A short time later, David came to Seattle for a visit. My youngest, Brittany, was going out with a guy who could not make a commitment. David felt led to talk to the boyfriend about looking at what was in front of him and not losing that opportunity. They talked for nearly two hours. Later, David said the first hour was about the boyfriend, and the rest was his realizing that he cared about me. He didn't sleep for three nights thinking about me.

Surprise, surprise, David eventually asked me out. When David called to ask if we could date, I was in Tucson, Arizona, on a golf trip with my ski club. My roommate was a nurse named Gale. While golfing I had gotten too close to a jumping cholla cactus. This type of cactus has invisible barbs that are long. I didn't think I was near the plant when I was retrieving my golf ball; however, they're called jumping cholla for a reason, and I ended up with four round balls of cactus on my butt. Gale was picking cactus off my butt when David called. David and I both knew we liked each other and knew each other's families. He had been around my kids. David was a Christian in practice. God really did answer my prayer to bring someone who fit me.

David and I got married on his birthday, May 23. My birthday is April 23, and his late wife's birthday was on December 23. So, 23 is "our" number.

We had many interests in common. He skied when he was growing up, so when we got married, he started skiing again. David and I love to travel. One of our travels took us to Australia.

We got on the plane in Seattle. I was looking at the airplane magazine. There was a place in the magazine that lists good doctors in various categories. I said to David, "Look. All the best doctors are from Maryland." There was John Brown, MD, Philip Jenkins, MD, and so on.

David gave me a weird look and said, "Sue, the MD stands for 'Medical Doctor' not Maryland." We had such a hard laugh about that. From then on, every time we get on a plane, he says we should look up the Maryland doctors. I'm fortunate we travel so well together, which is not always the case with spouses.

The Australia trip was fabulous. Before we went, we took classes to become certified as scuba divers. Our travels took us to Sydney, Melbourne, and Port Douglas. In Port Douglas, we dove in the Great Barrier Reef. The reefs are amazing with coral-like mountains. Such a great adventure.

Speaking of adventure, before David and I got married, I told him life would be an adventure with me. Shortly after marriage, I asked if he wanted to do something wild and crazy. His eyes lit up. "YEAH!" I think he may have been thinking along other lines...I took him to my nail salon for a pedicure!

He was uncomfortable at first, but he goes with me each time. David now knows why we gals like pedicures. But he was not sure it counted as an adventure, at least not the kind he was contemplating.

David and I are so connected that we say the same thing at the same time. In the middle of the night once we got up at the same time to go to the bathroom and bumped into each other at the end of the bed. We are the best of friends and give each other space when needed. We both love the Lord and regularly attend church.

David was raised with no religion. He was two when his mom divorced his dad. David never had any contact with his biological father after that. His stepdad adopted him and his brother Bill when David was four. Warren, his stepdad, is a secular Jew. When David married the first time, his new family was church going. David accepted Christ in the beginning of their marriage. They attended church regularly and raised their two daughters as Christians.

When David and I got together, we both believed our blessing was something only God could have orchestrated because many unrelated events had to happen for us to be together. The sequence gets complicated, but it illustrates why I think God steered me toward this wonderful man after four years of prayer for my fit.

- My son had to marry David's daughter.
- I had to be single when we met.
- David had to become a widower.
- We had to meet each other's family.
- All seven kids had to be on board with our dating.
- David had to be willing to sell his Colorado home and business and move 1,300 miles to Seattle.
- We had to completely fall in love.

Coincidence, you say? Definitely not. Clearly, God sure works in mysterious ways. Took Him long enough, though!

David and I are both retired and now skip Washington's rainy winters to spend our time in sunny Arizona. We have purchased a home in Arizona so David could once again see the sun during Seattle's soggy winter months. We both love Arizona and the friends we've made there. We have a wonderful church family and many activities. Golf is high on the list of our activities.

Since we have been together, we've discovered we are the best of friends and can spend time just enjoying each other's company. We work well together on projects around the house and yard. We are both hard workers.

When we got married, we decided I would oversee the household inventory, and he would take over repairs and maintenance. This arrangement works out well because whenever David is looking for any item, I usually know where it is. Having kids made me excellent at inventorying a room so I could always help find their stuff.

We did have some trouble in the first year of marriage because I tried to do everything by myself. I had been alone for so long, which meant I didn't even consider that David could help me. He is a wonderful organizer of space and stuff. He picks up after himself on projects. *AND* he does laundry and dishes.

In 2018, we decided to move out of Seattle proper due to the traffic and high taxes. A house in Lake Tapps near Tacoma, Washington, gives us a place for the summer to visit our 13 grandchildren.

We attend church every week with Christ being at the center of our beings. Praying together keeps us grounded.

David and I are living life to the fullest. We took a trip to Spain recently and loved the country. The food was so tasty. They have pastry shops on every corner. The Spaniards are friendly and helpful. The trip was a little hard for me because of all the walking. Still, I'm glad I went.

We had many talks during our strolls. I told him how I was feeling and how surreal it is to think I may not be here for the next holiday in that I still had cancer. I've been preparing for the inevitable for two years now, getting my estate in order and cleaning out stuff that I don't need. Spending time with the kids and grandkids has been a focus. I am proud that I taught my kids about having a personal relationship with God. I also instilled honesty, trust, and compassion for others.

Do I have many regrets? Sure. I wish I had started my personal relationship with God sooner. I wish hadn't worked so many hours for so many years.

But my remorse over those two things is overtaken by the good feeling I have that I took my kids on many adventures and created such colorful memories. We would just get in the car and go. They love to tell the story about the orange pop can.

We were headed to the state fair when one of the kids in the back seat wanted a sip of my Coke. I handed the can back. Pretty soon, they gave it back. I grabbed the can and took a swig. As soon as I did, I felt something bite my tongue. I spat and sputtered and almost drove off the road. Out came a live earwig! Earwigs have powerful pincers called forceps—a very accurate term.

The kids had handed back an old can of orange pop that had been sitting in the car for a few days because they wanted to keep the Coke. Of course, they didn't know the can contained a live resident leisurely sipping orange soda. They laughed all the way to the fair. Me too.

We would drive to the mountains, ocean, and Whistler. Trips usually involved some type of hiking in the woods or exploring distant towns. When the kids were young, I took them skiing by myself. Back then the tickets for kids were very reasonable. Even though it was difficult for me to get three little ones into their ski clothes and boots, I wanted my kids to have all types of sports experiences. They played tennis one summer. After Jon was gone, they all played baseball one summer. I would take them to the three separate fields, go back to watch each one, and then do the pickups. There was one time after I got home when things didn't feel right as I started the laundry. Then it hit me that I had forgotten to pick up Jarrod. Boy, was he mad when I pulled up in front of him and his coach sitting on the curb.

Sometimes my timing was off. There was a year that I made a reservation to go on an Alaskan cruise. My suitcase was packed, ready for a wonderful time exploring Alaska. I stepped to the check-in counter and was told my name wasn't on the list. The agent looked at my reservation papers and pronounced, "This is a cruise for NEXT year." Stunned, I asked if I could still get on the ship. Cruise lines won't allow last-minute passengers even if they have room. The reason has to do with clearing the credit card. I did take the Alaskan cruise twice in the following years, and it was wonderful.

CHAPTER 9

ANOTHER EMOTIONAL ROLLER COASTER

Shawn, my stepson, moved in with Jon and me on our wedding day in 1979. The kid's mother lived in Spokane, Washington. Shawn was 14 at the time. Dionne was 11. Teenagers are fun, but let's face it, they can be challenging. Part of that challenge comes about because they don't always consider the consequences of their actions.

For example, Shawn played basketball in high school. It was his passion. The problem I had with him was not basketball. I was happy he was so absorbed in a sport. It was his laundry habits that bugged me to death.

Shawn wore two pairs of socks to every practice and game. It wasn't bad enough that they smelled to high heaven right after he took them off, but he'd ball them, toss them in the hamper (probably a three-pointer), where they would marinate in his sweat until laundry day.

I didn't think I should be the only one to enjoy the heavenly Chanel N°5 scent emanating from his socks. So, one day, I called to him. "Hey, Shawn. Would you please bring me socks from your laundry hamper?"

He began rummaging around in the laundry basket. When he found them, he almost threw up. Then, I laid down the law. "Pull apart your socks after each wearing," I said sternly, "or you will be doing your own laundry from here on out." Nothing scares a teenage boy more than having to do laundry. That threat did the trick.

Shawn continued playing basketball into adulthood. It was only because he was having trouble with his balance being off that he stopped playing.

While not my biological son, Shawn was an easy kid to love. He blended into our new family so easily.

He was a typical teenage boy in many other ways too. I can see him standing at the water's edge with a piece of driftwood, hitting rocks into the water, which he did almost every day. At the other end of his habits, his room looked like a bomb had gone off in it. He frequently lost his car keys. To fix that problem, his grandmother got him a find-my-keys device. He lost that too.

When Shawn completed high school, he moved into a house

with some friends. He came home a few days later and said, "Mom, do you know how much milk costs!?" As if it was news to me.

"You bet I do," I said. "You always drank a ton of milk. Our food budget has gone way down since you moved out." It reminds me of the story about a kid who thought his parents got smarter and smarter the older he got.

Shawn also was fun. When Jarrod was two, Shawn was living next door to us at his grandmother's house. Jarrod and Shawn would wrestle and throw pillows for hours. Jarrod always came home dripping in sweat and loved every minute.

Shawn was a genuinely nice person. People gravitated toward him, and he was always kind. I liked his disposition very much. I spent years praying for him and gave him information about God. I often sent Bible passages to him. He always told me he was searching for but not ready to accept God.

One day I told him that in the Bible it talks about God knowing His children and their voice. The Bible talks about when it's too late to turn to God. There's a point when God will say, "My sheep hear my voice; I know them and they follow me" (John 10:27), which is supported by "I love the Lord because he hears my voice and my supplications" (Psalm 116:1).

IN JON'S FOOTSTEPS

Jon always led Shawn along all the right paths. Our Safety & Supply Company was Shawn's second home since he was around

15 when he started working there. He had done various jobs and had managed some departments in the company.

Jon and I set about teaching Shawn the ins and outs of everything. We mapped out a five-year plan to develop him for a leadership role in the company. Shawn was onboard with that goal.

He was in his 30s and married with two children when Jon died suddenly. Jon's death had a profound effect on Shawn. A year after Jon's death, Shawn went to stay at the hotel in that very same room. Perhaps he needed closure.

Jon's will stated that the company could go only to someone in the bloodline. Succession plans in family-run businesses are always dicey. I've read that only 30% of family-run enterprises survive the transition to a second generation and only 12% go on to the third. Shawn was the obvious and willing candidate.

To help him ease into the business, I made things more efficient and logical taxwise by blending my company with Jon's. I then made a sales agreement with Shawn for a 20-year buyout of the business at a very reasonable price. I did the buyout to honor Jon's direction that our company stay in the bloodline. Shawn was 36 at the time. He ran the company successfully until 2016 when he separated from his wife and began going through a difficult divorce.

In 2016 Shawn was diagnosed with ALS, Lou Gehrig's disease. This disease makes it hard to control your movements. Shawn's speech also was affected because it seemed his tongue got thick. He suffered from epilepsy since the age of 14. He had been dealing with alcoholism for some time, and all these issues compounded with the divorce were very hard on him.

The divorce dragged on for some time because his wife changed attorneys just as the matter was going to arbitration in July 2018. My voice was important during these negotiations because I wanted to honor Jon's directives of keeping the company in the family.

All parties should have signed the final divorce papers in 2019. Unfortunately, the final sign off was delayed for some reason. So even though the judge had signed off on the divorce settlement, Shawn and his wife's divorce stayed in limbo for quite a while.

In 2020 Shawn was living in an apartment in Oregon and hadn't gone to work for several days. The police went to his apartment to check on him but reported no problem because they could hear the TV. When he didn't show up at work again, his colleague and the police had the apartment manager let them into the apartment. On January 27, 2020, Shawn was found face down on the floor. According to the coroner, Shawn passed away from a seizure disorder. I am not sure if Shawn turned to God before he died. I am okay with that possibility only because I did what I could to tell him about God. I learned a long time ago that I can tell people my story and explain my faith. After that, I hold onto hope that I will see them in heaven.

Because the divorce decree had not been finalized at the

time of Shawn's death, his wife's attorney immediately vacated the divorce proceedings of the last three years as if they never happened. The result was that Shawn's widow received the company, the building, and all assets.

I was drowning in sadness that my stepson was getting divorced (something I'd hoped would never happen to any my kids), aching from his death, and unable to honor Jon's directive to keep the company within the bloodline. I felt anger and hurt because Jon and I had spent so many years building our company.

The last few years have been spent working through my anger on how all this tragedy ended. The disappointment in knowing I could not honor Jon's wishes affected me. I had to find a way to get over my anger.

I read a book called *Total Forgiveness* by R. T. Kendall that helped me forgive in my heart and feel comfortable again.

Forgiveness is for you and not the other person. Without forgiveness you can't heal your own heart. Bitterness and anger taint the way you look at life and fairness. These emotions wear on your mind and body and cause unseen stress. Stress can also bring on cancer or other diseases.

Total Forgiveness showed me that forgiveness does not have to involve keeping relationships. At first it was hard for me to go into the company building knowing she owned it. Because of forgiveness, I have let go of those emotions that had me anxious and frozen. God was always involved through prayer with my moving forward and helping me be okay with the way things turned out. My two granddaughters from Shawn are special to me, and I see them and pray for them. I do not have a relationship with Shawn's former wife but have forgiven her.

Shawn was part of my life for 40 years. I still miss him very much. His dad, Jon, died at 53, and now Shawn was gone at 54. That was way too young. More pain. These situations make me realize how life can change in the blink of an eye.

We don't know how long we will be on this earth. Every day should be cherished as a gift to spend with the people we love. Memories are more important than any of the stuff we acquire. I will always have fond memories of Shawn and the adventures we shared. I kinda miss the smell of those sweaty socks too.

CHAPTER 10

IT'S A GOD THING

So many coincidences have happened in my life that are too numerous to count. I have no explanation for them other than it's A God Thing. That expression has been prevalent in my life since I started my personal relationship with Him. Let me tell you some of my own "God Thing" stories.

MESSAGE FROM GOD

Writing the last chapter had a profound effect on me. During my writing, I discovered there was not total forgiveness in my heart. Two long nights were spent trying to figure out why so much anxiety was still at the surface. My insides were churning, and I couldn't sleep. On the second day, my prayers were asking God to help me figure out what was wrong with me.

God answered my prayers in a way I did not expect. Strong conviction told me that I had not actually grieved Shawn because of my feelings about the divorce. God told me to let those feelings go and grieve my son. God also told me clearly that I needed to move forward to reconcile with my daughter-in-law. His directive scared me but also gives me comfort that my heart will not hold any grudges. Grudges are relationship killers. I have one sister who won't talk to any of my family, including my mom. God told me I shouldn't model my sister's behavior because it is wrong. As I was explaining these revelations to my children, I broke down and started grieving Shawn. Grieving will take time, but I feel I need to reminisce about our past 40 years together. Whenever I told Shawn I loved him, he replied, "I love you more."

A God Thing.

BOATING WITH GOD

We lived on Puget Sound in Washington state. My second husband, Jon, wanted a boat so badly. But for many years, I would not let him get one because he was not mechanical at all. I knew *I* would end up diagnosing and fixing any problem. I wasn't up for that.

Well, dear reader, he wore me down, and finally in January 2000, we went to the boat show and picked out a 21-ft. Sea Ray Cuddy Cabin. It wasn't huge, but it had a berth for sleeping. We named it Tequila Sunrise after our two cats. Our house didn't have a dock to tie up the boat, so we would attach the rope to a buoy (floating ball) that was secured to a cement block resting on the ocean floor. We would then row out to the boat in a Zodiac, a rigid, inflatable raft, and board the boat.

We took the delivery of the boat in March; Jon died in April.

I didn't know the first thing about boats or maintenance or navigation rules or anything. I knew what a barnacle was, but that was about it. I was your classic landlubber.

So, I found Bob, a trustworthy seaman, by way of Google, who could teach us how to handle the boat.

The day arrived for our first lesson. I, along with Jarrod, his friend Nick, and Nick's father donned our lifejackets and climbed into our brand-spanking-new seagoing yacht—er, boat.

Wouldn't you know it? The very first time we tried to start it up, there was nothing but silence from the engine. Bob came to the rescue and announced it was nothing more than the boat fuse. Weird, since that's pretty uncommon, he said, and there were no extras on board. Nick and his dad stepped off the boat and went to buy a new fuse. Not wanting to waste time, I asked Bob to show me the ins and outs of the engine. Learn everything now, I thought, because you may be stuck miles from land and need to know this very information.

We were both deep into a discussion about air flow and proper oiling techniques when suddenly Jarrod yelled, "Mom, there's a huge wave coming!" I jerked my head up to see a wall of water coming at us. We hadn't even been out in our new boat when this mini tsunami came barreling down on us. Would Tequila Sunrise survive the onslaught? Would *we*?

Luckily, our little craft rocked and heaved, but we rode out the swell. My heart didn't stop pounding for several minutes. Our neighbor's Boston Whaler didn't fare as well. It had flipped upside down, leaving the boat's console buried in the sand. Imagine if I'd been sleeping in our boat and this huge wave had come during the night. I would have thought the world was ending.

When I realized we weren't in any more danger, I looked out to sea and saw a freighter in the distance. The freighter had (illegally) sped through the shipping lane causing the wave. I wanted to go out there and give the captain of that vessel what-for. Or at least get some identification of the ship so I could report it to the authorities. But all I could do was call my neighbor to deliver the bad news about her upside-down craft.

Bob jumped on this timely opportunity to show me how to use the radio to call for help: Mayday! Mayday!

We also had a lesson on how to dock the boat and many other need-to-know boating issues, like not bringing any alcohol aboard, wearing our life jackets 100% of the time, heeding buoy markers, going slowly when near the dock, and watching for logs and wildlife.

In some respects, navigation rules are like those for driving. You may technically have the right of way, but the ultimate goal is to drive so that everyone is safe. Not wanting to ram into anyone, I decided that *everyone else* would have the right of way. On this initial trip, at least, I left the driving to Bob and Jarrod.

At the end of the day, Bob wanted to take me out for sandwiches. Looking back, I wondered if this was God trying to send me another love interest. But Bob's invitation was so close to Jon's death that I was probably too out of it to even know a guy was coming on to me. I declined, but the kids forever called him "Bob, the Boat Guy Who Wanted to Date Mom."

I modified my penchant for adventure a bit after that pretty jarring start to my boating career by almost capsizing! Too bad Jon hadn't been there to rock 'n' roll with us that day.

I did, however, become the Queen of Lost Buoys on our beach. Our first buoy was a three-prong setup with a cement block on the sea floor coming up to one rope attached to the buoy. After the summer, boats have to be taken off the water when the storms come; buoys are usually left in the water. That buoy disappeared during the coming winter. Three years later that first buoy bobbed back up. It had gone over the drop-off, where the sea floor went down to around 400 feet, which is why it could be a shipping lane. In between those years, the buoy must have become hung up on edge of the drop-off and was only shaken loose three years later.

Meanwhile, it was time for a new buoy. The second buoy was attached to a 1,300-pound concrete block at the shelf edge. It was supposed to have a galvanized chain, but it was not galvanized, so it rusted out during the winter. My neighbor had to scuba dive to attach a new galvanized chain. He told me to pull the chain into the shore at the end of the season so that we would find it for next year. I spent hours up to my chest in the water with a rake trying to locate that chain. My neighbor also looked for it with no luck.

My decision was to move the boat to a slip at Lake Union. When the kids got older, I sold the boat.

A God Thing.

THE HOUSE OF THE LORD

After Jon died, I would visit my neighbor Gladys whose husband, Howard, had passed. My kids and I had been visiting them regularly for years. After Howard died, Gladys was alone and not able to drive. I was at her house one day when she burst into tears. She said her son had told her to sell her house and move in with his family. She was so upset because she and her husband had built the house and raised their family there. The thought of having the next owner knock it down upset her so much she was beside herself with heartbreak over that too.

God put that dilemma on my heart. So, I hatched a plan that worked out a little differently than I had expected. I had a little insurance money, so I made an offer on her house. She took my offer, but we had not closed yet.

Then my mom called to say she and my dad had been broken into *while at home*! The thieves put a ladder up to the third story window and brazenly came downstairs to steal my mom's purse and dad's wallet.

She was understandably upset and feared there would be another break-in. That's when I hatched yet another great idea. I told her about the house I was buying and asked if they would want to move into a one-story house in a better neighborhood. She agreed, but it took nine months for my dad to come around. Gladys picked the closing date for the house, which happened to be my mom's birthday.

The upside from all these events was having Dad and Mom clean out their three-story house and downsize. That chore was something on the horizon anyway. So it was the perfect time to go through their belongings and decide what to throw out, keep, and donate. Otherwise, we kids would have had to do it eventually. The other good news was that I was also four doors away, so I could help them.

I didn't know why I made the offer to buy the house. But God did. My parents lived there for 13 years until my dad's dementia became unmanageable for my mom, which meant moving them into a special facility. My sweet neighbor who had loved that house so dearly was very touched when she heard about my mom's tender, loving care of the house and yard. I didn't make any changes to the house until after I learned that Gladys had passed away at age 103.

A God Thing.

GOLFING WITH GOD

My friend Julie now plays pickleball with our church group. She had not been in a church family or accepted Christ as her Savior. Julie had been invited by a friend to play pickleball. One day we had a workday at church. She joined three of us weeding the garden in the back. One woman was telling my friend her story of finding Christ. After our day together, I went to Julie and asked her if anyone had ever asked if she wanted to accept Christ as her Savior. She started crying and said she wanted to but didn't know how.

I walked her through what it means to be a child of God. She repented her sins and asked Christ into her life as her Savior. We all prayed. Some weeks later, she wanted to get baptized on a day when her college-age daughter and two sons could attend. She asked me to attend the ceremony.

She confided in me that she worried how her college-age kids would like the pastor and the church. As it happened, the Tuesday before the baptism, her two sons decided to play golf on an afternoon at a course they had never been on. They were randomly assigned to play with a third golfer. Around hole two, Eric, the younger son, asked this man if he was from Arizona. He said no. He had moved there from Tennessee. "I am Brian Jobe, a pastor at a church called Compass," he told the boys—the same church as their mother's baptism. Eric asked if he knew a person named Julie in his congregation.

The pastor said, "Why, yes. I'm baptizing Julie on Sunday!"

The boys had a wonderful round of golf with this preacher and were overjoyed because they knew their mom was in good hands. Julie showed me a picture of her sons and our pastor at the golf course. Now my friend finally understood what it meant when we girls told her it was A God Thing.

HITCHHIKING WITH CANCER

One day driving back from taking my daughter to school in the pouring rain, I saw a woman running for a bus. She missed it by a hair. I knew that frustration all too well and could see she was completely exhausted and upset. Couldn't the driver have waited just one more second, especially when he saw her running?

I pulled over, rolled down my window, and asked, "Need a ride?"

She looked so grateful at my kindness, climbed in, closed her sopping umbrella, and asked if I would take her to the next bus stop. Phooey on that! I ended up driving her downtown to her office.

It wasn't that far. We started talking, as women do, and guess what: She had just been diagnosed with breast cancer.

Five million things ran through my mind that I wanted to tell her now that I had just gone through my treatment. But I also didn't want to overwhelm her. I answered all her questions and reassured her that this woe too would pass. She hugged me and thanked me profusely for picking her up. I think about her often.

A God Thing.

GOD IN THE NURSING HOME

I was visiting my mother at her assisted-living place. It was summertime and blazing hot. I saw a girl waiting at the bus stop on my way in. I visited Mom for about an hour then left to go home. On my way out, I saw the same girl still at the bus stop. I rolled down my window and asked if she wanted a ride. She couldn't get into my air-conditioned car fast enough. Turns out she worked at the same facility where my mom lived.

She asked my mother's name and when I answered she said, "I know Bev. She likes tea."

Her speech seemed a little slow and simple. So, it didn't surprise me when she recounted a story about sustaining a brain injury in a serious car accident at 17. She shared that she lived next door to her parents, so they and her husband helped her. She had been working at the facility for many years. Very sweet girl. I was glad she took such good care of my mom.

A God Thing.

GOD'S DOG

My daughter Brittany had signed up to visit a retirement community, the Kenney Home, for her senior volunteer project. I decided to accompany her and help where I could.

I asked the staff member to suggest a resident to visit. She pointed me toward Frances, who had moved to Seattle with her ailing husband at the behest of her daughter.

"Frances is very withdrawn," the employee said. Her husband had passed away in April of that year.

I knocked on Frances's door, introduced myself, and asked if she wanted some company. She recounted some memories of her husband. But the employee was right: She was withdrawn. When I said my husband had died in April (but a few years earlier), she knew I would understand about her pain and opened up about her feelings.

We met a few more weeks. Then out of the blue, she mentioned how much she missed having dogs. I knew the solution to that problem.

The next time I went, I smuggled Beau, my Yorkshire terrier, into her apartment, which was very much against the rules. He ran over, jumped in her lap, and kissed her on the cheek. Beau then hopped on her couch to take a nap. Frances loved Beau. I eventually got him certified so I could bring him every week. We would visit Frances and others. In fact, I took Beau to visit the residents every week for three years. After three years, my work schedule changed so I had to stop my visits.

Everyone in the Kenney Home loved my Yorkie. He wasn't scared of anyone and just sat patiently while people petted him. There was so much joy on people's faces.

Eventually I asked the staff if I could take Frances to dinner. They said her daughter would have to okay it. The daughter was delighted that someone was taking an interest in her mom but somewhat apprehensive.

I got a big surprise when I finally met this daughter. She was the grandmother of kids that lived a few houses from me. From then on, we all went to dinner, and I was invited to every event they had for their mom.

I also visited a woman who had lost her whole family: Both her husband and two kids had died. Betty never had any visitors. She was very lonely, and I think I made a difference in her life for those three years.

Another resident named Shirley had multiple sclerosis and could only move her head and one hand a little bit. Shirley had been in this state for three years before I started visiting her. Beau would sit close to her on the bed, and she would tell me about her life. She had divorced when divorce was less than acceptable. Shirley had two boys but only one would visit her. There were ladies from her church who came regularly. After Shirley passed away, her son called to tell me how much his mother loved our visits.

A God Thing.

ZERO DEGREE OF SEPARATION FROM GOD

David used to say that I was one degree of separation from people when most people are five or six degrees away from others. I am always running into people I know in the weirdest places. I had a classmate who was a football player, a famous quarterback for Washington State University. I ran into him *twice* in Hawaii. I think if you have your eyes open and not focused on yourself (or your phone), you increase the chances of having amazing experiences.

That is, your own God Things.

GOD SAYS USE IT OR LOSE IT

Jarrod had a Holy Spirt moment and felt the need to take food and a Bible verse to homeless people. He picked out Matthew 25:14-30, the parable of the talents, which urges people to use what God has given us to bring Him glory and honor. Jarrod went to church with me that Sunday. Guess what the sermon was based on. Yup. Matthew 25:14-30.

A God Thing.

SHARING THE PAIN

I was in Walgreens recently wearing my shirt from the Alki 5K run to support breast cancer. As I walked by, a woman mentioned my shirt and said she had lived in West Seattle for many years. This woman, Audrey, told me her husband had passed away two months ago. I said I had also lost my husband many years ago. Audrey felt comfortable enough to tell me about her life and her husband's passing. I asked Audrey if I could give her a hug. The tears in her eyes said everything. Being a good listener is a gift from God, and I use it to the best of my ability.

A God Thing.

A GIFT FOR A MOM

Watching a young mom with three small children try to finish her shopping in Target brought me back to my own experience with little ones. The woman's youngest was crying loudly. I could see the exhaustion on her face. I stopped and said, "Being a mom is really hard some days, so I want you to have this gift just to do something for yourself." I handed her a $25 gift card, and she started crying. I always carry a few gift cards with me and pay attention to those around me for opportunities to bless another person.

A God Thing.

GOD'S MIGHTY PEN

My dad taught me the power of writing letters to correct processes that are not working. My kids tease me about it, but the joke's on them because my letters get results. For example, I worked for three years to help Seattleites report crimes online.

David and I had a new fishing boat backed up to our garage. We lived on a dead-end street in the city. One night, thieves cut the fuel and electric lines and took our new $3,800 trolling motor off the boat. At the time, one could only report thefts up to $500 online. If over $500, a detective had to give you the case number to file an insurance claim. It took three months and going into the precinct to finally get a case number for our insurance claim. I called and wrote to the chief of police about the wasted time of detectives and their inability to help us in a timely manner.

I'm proud to say they finally changed their policy, so any dollar amount of theft can be reported online.

A God Thing.

GRIEF HAS A THOUSAND LIVES

The year after Jon's death was very hard for my family. The year before, Jon had gone off to work on a business trip and never came home. In 2001, on September 11 (the date of the infamous 9/11 attack on the twin towers in New York), my mind went right back to that overwhelming fear I experienced when I realized that I would never see Jon again or talk to him. So many people experienced the same reality on September 11. My heart was breaking for all who lost loved ones. No matter the distance in time and place, we all are connected.

A God Thing.

KEEPING TRACK (SO GOD DOESN'T HAVE TO)

David and I work so well together. I keep our goals on Notes in my phone. If we are driving any length of time, we go over our goals. When a goal is achieved, I move it down in the note to COMPLETED. We have a clear picture of what we are working toward and what we have accomplished. I heard once that if you write goals down you have a much higher chance of completion because the goal is visible. With God in your life, it is amazing what you can accomplish.

A God Thing.

"BEARLY" MAKING IT OUT ALIVE

David and I love adventure. We had gone to Whistler in British Columbia, Canada, during one summer with our ski club for a week. David loves trail and mountain biking while I prefer paved trails to ride on. David will go into the hills and come back to me periodically. I was riding around a corner just as David was coming off the hill. There was a black bear right in front of me, so I had to stop quickly. David told me to get off my bike slowly while he made a lot of noise and made himself look as big as possible to scare the bear. The bear looked at him and sauntered back into the woods. I'm glad I wasn't alone for that ride!

A God Thing.

GOD'S GOOD WILL

After Jon died, I was packing to move to another house and cleaning out closets, etc. For the life of me, I couldn't find several pieces of jewelry Jon had given me, among them a stunning black-pearl necklace from Kauai. I went through pockets and drawers and turned my bedroom upside down. Nothing.

I had gathered a whole carload of bags for Goodwill, but when I got there, it was closed.

When I got back home, I unloaded the bags back into the

garage. Soon thereafter, my granddaughter Olivia noticed a pair of black cowboy boots with flowers up the side.

"Nana, can I try on these boots?" she asked, picking them out of the bag.

"Sure," I said.

But when she put her foot into one, she said, "Hey, Nana. I can't get it on. There's a sock in here!"

I turned the boot upside down and out came a Tiffany's bag with all the jewelry I had been searching for.

Olivia looked at me and said sheepishly, "Nana, please don't be mad at me, but I may have put that in there when I was little."

If Goodwill had not been closed, someone would have found those precious and very expensive pieces of jewelry.

A God Thing.

THE KEY TO GOOD HEALTH

I had a separate set of keys for the office. They were misplaced for weeks. I searched and searched for them with no luck. I asked God for help because I really needed to find those darn keys.

One day, when I was going to the gym, I picked up my gym bag and for some reason my attention was directed to an inside zipper pocket. I opened the pocket—there were the keys. Everyone was looking at me as I exclaimed, "Thank you, Lord!"

A God Thing.

PAYING GOD'S LOVE FORWARD

I was in the doctor's office with my three kids. After Brittany's birth, I was more attuned to people around me and always had an ear open. There was a woman I heard talking to the receptionist about getting her disability form signed.

The receptionist told her she would have to pay her outstanding bill before they would sign the paperwork. The women left, and a few minutes later came back in crying and plunked down in a chair. I looked over and realized it was a woman who used to work at my kids' daycare.

I went up to the desk and asked if I could pay her bill. The bill was not very much, and I paid it so that she could get her form signed.

A few years later, I ran into this woman when I started community college. She thanked me again for helping her and told me she was almost done with her school program so she would be able to get a good job. I often wonder what would have happened to her if I had not paid the bill for her.

I had started going to the same college to get a bachelor's degree in business management. Graduation came for me at age 53.

The first 18 months were before cancer with the last 18 months after chemo. Chemo brain is a true disability, so I was proud of myself for finishing.

A God Thing.

SLEEPING SOUNDLY

I was in Target around Christmas time. The person behind me was holding new pajamas for a teen.

I said, "Oh, someone is getting new jammies for Christmas."

"They're not a Christmas gift," she said. "It's going to be pajama day at my daughter's school. I have to buy her something. I just can't afford them now."

I handed her a gift card that would pay for those pajamas. She broke down in tears.

A God Thing.

CONNECTIONS ARE EVERYWHERE!

Early on in our neighborhood Bible study group, we discovered that three of us had lived in the *same house* in Three Tree Point! It was a basement apartment in a two-story house. Betty was one in our Bible study group who was living in the house then, so I went to see where Bill and I had lived after our marriage.

That visit shook loose one memory from 50 years before.

My unemployed, snoozy husband got out of bed one morning and almost tripped over a dead rat in the bedroom doorway. Obviously, my cat had been hard at work during the night and brought in his "present" to show us, as cats do. I thought it was funny.

My husband didn't. He called me at work to complain.

"It's disgusting, and because the cat is yours, *you* can dispose of it."

So, the rat lay on the floor all day. By the time I got home, rigor mortis had set in. I took a paper towel, picked up the stiff carcass, and threw it in the trash. Then I thanked my cat for ridding the world of another one of these disease-carrying vermin.

A God Thing.

IT'S A SMALL WORLD!

I had purchased a condo in West Seattle for rental purposes. One of my tenants called me from a number that said New Ulm. I found out she had been raised in that small German town in Minnesota, the very same town where my mom had grown up. I'd also spent many summers there visiting my relatives. Coincidence or...

A God Thing.

THANK GOD FOR GENEALOGY

This is an improbable and convoluted story about our family.

My grandfather, Axel Olson, married Christina Olson in Minnesota on April 16, 1924, and started a family of five, except that one child, Ruth, died a few days after birth. My dad was 16 when his father, Axel, committed suicide. World War I had left Axel disabled because he had been gassed with chlorine gas at Cantigny, France, in July 1918. Axel was in the 1st Division and the first American unit to occupy the front without British or French support. They held Cantigny through seven counter attacks by the Bosches. The word Bosches is a French word meaning rascal or German as found on a Google search. Axel was discharged 75% disabled on May 5, 1919. The information here was part of a newspaper article announcing his return home. We never knew much about Axel's history until around 2003.

A relative from Sweden contacted my dad to say he wanted to visit us in the U.S. This man had been doing genealogy and tracked down my father to tell him the story of one of our long-lost relatives Axel Guldbrandsson.

Here's the story: A man in Sweden named Erik Mansson, my great-grandfather, worked at a lumber mill. Erik Mansson fell in love with the mill owner's younger daughter, Karolina Guldbrandsson. Erik asked the mill's owner for Karolina's hand in marriage, but he said no because she was too young; Erik would have to marry the older daughter, as that was the custom back then. So, Erik reluctantly married Marta. In the meantime, he also built a house for Karolina on the other side of the road. He wanted to have his cake and eat it too.

Erik and Marta had nine children. Erik and Karolina had eight, including my grandfather, Axel. Those eight were born out of wedlock, so their baptismal records were marked "bastard," including Axel's. Unfortunately, two of Karolina's children passed away. Karolina was very poor, and after Erik and Marta had moved away, Karolina and her children had to move in with her brother.

When my grandfather, Axel, came to the U.S. at age 19, the authorities at Ellis Island apparently changed the spelling of his last name from Guldbrandsson to Olson. Perhaps it was too difficult to spell or pronounce. We would have never known this story but for this relative in Sweden who serendipitously found us on the internet.

If not for Erik and his love for the younger daughter, I would not be here. God is present even in our most twisted family stories.

A God Thing.

SITTING AT GOD'S TABLE

When we moved from Seattle, we brought with us a large dining table that was way too big for our new house. After two years, we found a smaller table that worked great. It even had a leaf we could add for bigger crowds. My husband put the too-big table and chairs in our driveway and posted a sign that said, "For sale $300." Zero bites. After three days of schlepping it into the garage in the evening and back out the next day, I said, "Take down the for-sale sign and mark it 'Free' because I am going to let God decide who gets it."

Soon thereafter, a woman stopped by and said she loved the dining set and that her son would come by to pick it up. It turned out she lived just one block over. She confided that she had recently gone through treatment for breast cancer. Did we talk about that topic or what! She said she also loved the Lord. We had so many things in common. We will definitely be spending more time together.

A God Thing.

GOD AND VENMO

As I was waiting to pay for picture frames in Hobby Lobby, I heard the woman in front of me chatting animatedly with the clerk about how excited her husband would be to get the items she was buying for his birthday. But when she tried using Apple Pay, the cashier said Hobby Lobby didn't accept that form of payment. She rummaged around in her purse for her credit card and became more and more distressed when she couldn't find it. "Oh, dear, I guess I'll have to put these things back."

She gathered up the items and turned to put them back when I said, "I'll pay for them," and took out my wallet.

She looked so relieved. "Let me pay your back. Do you have Venmo?"

I waved her off. "I try to do something nice for someone every day," I said. "Today is your day!"

By this time, the clerk was dabbing at her eyes with a tissue. The picture frames I was buying turned out to be half off, which more than paid for the $46 I paid for that woman's purchase. You can never out-give God! The clerk was still tearing up when she finished the transaction. "That was so wonderful," she said.

A God Thing.

GOD IN THE ICU

My dad was having trouble breathing, so we took him to Harborview Medical Center in Seattle. He was admitted to the intensive care unit. We were about to leave when I ran into Linda, a member of our ski club and lead nurse for respiratory cases. She and I had talked previously about my dad, so when she saw us, she assured me she would check in on my dad periodically. It made me feel so much better.

A God Thing.

GOD IN THE NEIGHBORHOOD

Among my neighbors when I lived in Seattle, I had one in particular, Barb, for many years. She was widowed shortly before my husband died. Barb found out I had cancer again. Turns out she has a cousin who lives near us in Lake Tapps, Washington. The cousin's wife has metastatic breast cancer and is two years ahead of me in her cancer journey. Barb gave me Anita's information, and we'd meet for coffee to support each other. This introduction has been such a blessing to me and Anita. Having the exact same disease in common, both being Christians, and living near each other is a gift from God.

A God Thing.

I am happy to share my stories. Please share some of your own "A God Thing" tales!

Email: suzanne@suzannemurrayauthor.com

CHAPTER 11

RECIPE FOR PERSONAL WELL-BEING AND ENHANCING INTERACTION WITH OTHERS

1. Smile often: When I smile just a little at other people, they often talk to me because I seem inviting to them. I have heard many stories from people who needed to have someone listen to them.

2. Listen and look: Sometimes you can help in a small way. Examples are opening the door, helping a mom put the grocery cart away after she puts her kids in the car, acknowledging those who serve you (grocery checkers), calling them by name, and asking how their day is going.

3. Stay positive: People can learn to be positive in their circumstances. Positivity takes practice, and I would invite all of you to do one positive thing a day. After this step

becomes natural, add more positivity. Tracking positivity will make you feel good about yourself and could help someone else in a huge way.

4. Keep the faith: My faith brings me a contentment that is not possible without faith. Find a church and meet some friends.

5. Get involved: So many people are lonely today. Neighbors don't know each other. Many people don't leave their houses very often. Explore ways you can help in your local community. Years ago, when I was taking my small Yorkie pup to that nursing home, the staff asked me to bring him to the hospital area to visit a woman who was near death. She wanted to see my dog, so I put Beau near her face. She got the biggest smile and pointed to her forehead. She told me she would remember it forever. The woman died the next morning.

6. Reach out: Social media is a great way to find others who've faced a crisis like yours. Look for groups online that could help you or use your experience to help them weather their own storm.

7. Meet up: Find activities you like to do. Mine were skiing and golf. Instead of sitting at home, I joined a ski club and a women's golf club. My kids were in their late teens and didn't want to spend time with me anymore, so I needed to find some friends. Join a book club, gardening club, or find a group for outdoor activities like hiking or

biking. There are many free activities and groups to join. Activities make you feel good about yourself.

8. Take care: Take a hot bath. Be intentional about what makes you happy and calm. Go on a walk. Watch the sunset. Read a good book. Do something good to get your mind off your troubles and self-pity.

9. Make phone calls: Call folks who may need you more than you need them. Make the call to those you know will give you solid feedback and encouragement on your journey of healing.

10. Pray: Ask God for comfort, strength, healing, wisdom. Read about resilient women in your Bible.

11. Journal: Writing down our thoughts and feelings is a sure-fire way to gain perspective. It's free therapy!

12. If appropriate, get professional help.

CHAPTER 12

LETTER TO MY 18-YEAR-OLD SELF

Dear Younger Me,

Be still. You really can relax and enjoy yourself without having to move so quickly. The future is uncertain, so be true to your God and your values. Watch out for evil, as there are evil people in our world. Trust, but maybe with a little bit of caution. God will be there to pick up the pieces if you make mistakes. You are allowed to make a few and learn from them.

Be happy and content as much as possible. It is not someone else's job to provide your happiness. By having a strong relationship with God, you will have strength and wisdom to make good choices. Do not rush into something because you think that is what is expected of you. Always pray and wait before making big, life-changing moves. Seek advice from older people who may know more and have more experience than you.

You can decide how you respond to any crisis. Maybe choose

to see the experience as a learning event. Use those experiences to grow and help others grow. Always share with others.

Be humble as you go into adulthood. You should never feel that you are better than another person. Don't judge others, as that is God's job. It is more than likely that you don't have their full story.

OTHER RANDOM THOUGHTS

Perfection is a blessing but also a curse. As the second child and oldest girl in my birth family, I naturally took on a role of responsibility. I would help my mom with the four younger girls. My youngest sister, Kristin, was my very own baby doll. I was 10 and loved playing with dolls, so it was natural for me to take her as a live version of my play dolls. Family pictures show that I always had Kristin with me. I wouldn't change anything about how I took care of her and loved her so much. Kristin feels like I was her mom.

My kindergarten report card shows I always finished my work and played well with others. I was born an optimist.

Back to perfection. I worked many hours a week during my career because of my perfectionism. I loved work and felt a great sense of accomplishment with work. My employees were respected by me and given a chance to learn and improve. It was very important to me that employees learned that mistakes were an opportunity to correct processes. What I didn't respect was an employee who tried to blame someone else for their goof-ups. Don't do that.

I used to watch "Fly Lady" on the internet. She is an organizer who helps people keep their houses clean without going crazy. I really liked a phrase she used, "It's okay to vacuum in the middle." In other words, just get it done. You don't have to move all the furniture all the time.

Perfection can mean you are not delegating enough work to others. It's a mirage that only you can make things perfect. I had to learn to assign tasks to others and let go of that perfectionist nonsense so that other people could grow. It hasn't been easy to let go. I continue to practice delegating almost every day.

All parts of life lead to experiences that form your personality. I would probably wait to get married the first time. I also should have waited before marrying The Con. I should have relied on prayer and patience in those instances. As a type-A personality, my M.O. was always "Move forward and get it done." Impatience is not good for seeing all sides of an issue. Woulda. Coulda. Shoulda.

After being lied to in my first marriage, I was not as trusting. However, after a 20-year second marriage, the death of my husband left me vulnerable. Luckily, I did a prenup before marrying The Con. Betrayal hurts and stays with a person. I was shocked with myself for believing The Con and falling for his lies. I do wonder if I had waited just a little bit longer after Jon died if I would have been taken in so easily. But then, The Con preyed on vulnerable widows for that very reason.

Today I have a strong faith and trust God with my future. Not knowing how long I have left to live is a new experience. I can't help but think, "Will I be here next Christmas?"

"Do I have my life in order, so it won't be hard to process my estate?"

"How will my kids do without me?"

"How will David do?" He has already lost a wife to cancer.

All in all, I have had a wonderful life with many exciting adventures. I told my kids if I go early, I will have won the "heaven lottery," meaning I lived way past all my doctors' expectations with my condition. I will have won God's promise of eternal life in paradise where there will be no evil or tears.

I want to be remembered as a person who loved Jesus, helped others, and lived a joyful life. I want people to know that memories are more important than stuff.

Recently, I heard that when you have a child, you only have 18 summers to raise them. Those summers go by so quickly. Please spend as much time as possible staying attuned to your loved ones and those around you. God can use you in a powerful way if you just open up to amazing experiences in helping others.

Made in the USA
Las Vegas, NV
28 March 2024

87927232R00085